EDUCATIONAL TECHNOLOGY

EDUCATIONAL TECHNOLOGY

Knowledge Assessment

Editor
Marmar Mukhopadhyay

SHIPRA

(2010, First Published 2004)

Rs. 995; US$ 35

ISBN: 978-81-7541-180-7

2014 impression

Educational Technology: Knowledge Assessment

Published by:

SHIPRA PUBLICATIONS
LG 18-19, Pankaj Central Market,
I.P. Ext., Patparganj, Delhi 110092, India
Ph.: +91 1147322068, 9650028065, 9810522367
Email: info@shiprapublication.com
www.shiprapublication.com

Preface

Teacher salary anywhere in the world is the highest single item of expenditure in education. It is not without reason hence that all over the world, a massive investment is made on research in teaching-learning. It makes equally good sense in investing the 'scholar-energy' on educational technology that is concerned with optimizing human learning. For, teaching-learning is the central core of the educational system.

Deeper understanding of human brains and the way we learn simultaneously with developments in information and communication technology have ushered in a paradigm shift in educational technology. Important developments in a variety of fields are continuously shaping educational technology. New knowledge is being created. Globally, knowledge utilization, however, has not been able to keep pace with knowledge creation resulting into huge loss of meaningful opportunities of optimizing human learning. The magnitude of the gap between knowledge creation and knowledge utilization seems to be directly related to developmental level of the society; gap is wider in the relatively less developed countries.

There is a vast and high quality literature on educational technology; and the literature is steadily growing through a variety of sources. It is necessary to take account from time to time of current knowledge in selected aspects of educational technology including the state of the art of knowledge utilization and estimated gaps between knowledge development and knowledge utilization. In continuation to such knowledge assessment, to facilitate better utilization in future, it is equally important to project likely developments in educational technology in the near future. This book addresses selected issues in educational technology from this knowledge assessment perspective. It covers a wide range of theoretical issues and practical applications like evolution of educational technology, instructional design, communication, video-conferencing, hyper-media, online education, multi-channel learning, open and distance education, evaluation of educational technology, etc.

And, in this extraordinary journey of knowledge assessment in educational technology, scholars of great repute from several countries have joined me. I must acknowledge, with sincere thanks, their contributions. I hope my readers will find the book as exciting as I found conceptualizing, organizing, and editing it.

27 December, 2003 **Marmar Mukhopadhyay**
New Delhi

Contents

1

Evolution of Educational Technology

MARMAR MUKHOPADHYAY

Educational Technology under different names and notions has travelled a long-distance down the corridors of history. The Western scholars trace it down to the 1600s with the works of Comenius, particularly his book *"The World of Visuals"*. Educational technology in its basic spirit and form can be traced to much earlier days in the older civilizations like India, China and Egypt. *The Upanishads*, particularly *Sikshavalli* in *Taitteriya Upanishad*, I and many other ancient works sheds light on what we call educational technology, today.

The long gestation and wide spread application of educational technology raises several important questions. Is educational technology a major professional field of activity? Can it be considered as a discipline? Can people working in educational technology bc called as educational technologists and as a specialist group of professionals. In this chapter, an effort has been made to trace the history of educational technology as it evolved over the years, and finally examine its place in human knowledge systems as a specialist field.

The Concept of Educational Technology

There have been some meaningful efforts in defining educational technology, though consensus is yet to arrive. Understandably, since it is still evolving, it poses problems in being amenable to a precise definition. Its basic parameters, however, particularly its objectives and goals and its place in the overall educational system, are known and acceptable.

Joint Director, NIEPA, New Delhi, India

The Definition and Terminology Committee of AECT (1972) presented the following definition:

"Educational Technology is a field involved in the facilitation of human learning through the systematic identification, development, organization, and utilization of a full range of learning resources, and through the management of these process. It includes, but is not limited to, the development of Instructional Systems, the identification of existing resources, the delivery of resources to learners, and the management of these process and the people performing them..."

It is systems approach, deployment of full range of learning resources and organization of learning processes synthesized into total approach to facilitate learning, that create the uniqueness of and thus the rationale for, the field of educational technology. The AECT, in 1977, provided a new statement broadening the definition of educational technology:

"Educational Technology is a complex, integrated process involving people, procedures, ideas, devices, and organization, for analyzing problems and devising, implementing, evaluating, and managing solutions to those problems, involved in all aspects of human learning".

Such definitions tend to take us to contend that the basic purpose of educational technology is optimizing human learning implying 'economics of learning'. "The major concern in education today is the widening gap between learning potential and learning outcome. In a conventional sense this amounts to underachievement. Underachievement today is widespread and almost all pervasive at all levels of education and training. The non-correspondence between learning potential and outcome is universal but far more acute in countries like ours, since educational processes and methods continue unaltered on the face of changing techniques and technologies in the non formal learning and learning of life skills outside the four walls of schools and colleges. If educational technology has any quarrel with the conventional system it is on this ground. The birth of educational technology is for optimizing human learning through new unconventional learning techniques" (Mukhopadhyay, 1993).

Reiser (1987) quotes Definitions of Instructional Technology by the Commission on Instructional Technology (1970):

"Instructional technology can be defined in two ways. In its more familiar sense, it means *the media born of the communications revolution which can be used for instructional purposes alongside the teacher, textbook, and blackboard* ..... The pieces that make up instructional technology [include]: television, films, over-head projectors, computers, and other items of "hardware" and "software" ..."

Educational technology has been described as an the interactive output of technology of education and technology in education (Percival and Ellington, 1984)—technology of education as the scientific aspects of educational processes, and technology in education is the technology or the artifacts used by the teachers. The educational technology is seen as the interactive output where technology of educational provides the conceptual framework, technology in education provides the support to convert those concepts into practice.

History of Educational Technology

There have been several important efforts in tracing the history of evolution of educational technology earlier. The first and the most important work is by Seattle in 1966 in his book *"The History of Educational Technology"*. Michael Eraut's chapter in the *"International Encyclopedia of Educational Technology"* edited by Michael himself is another important document on the subject. One of the most exhaustive treatment to the subject has been provided by Reiser in his chapter, "The concept and evolution of educational technology" in the book *"Instructional Technology: Foundation"* edited by Robert M. Gagne in 1987. Another comparatively recent exercise is by the Swiss author, Brdicka. Others who have contributed in one way or the other are D.P. Ely in the *"International Encyclopedia of Education"*, and S.S. Kulkarni in his book *"Introduction to Educational Technology"*. I have traced the development of educational technology in India in *Encyclopedia of Indian Education* (in press).

There are two major trends in tracing the history of educational technology. Both Reiser as well as Eraut traced the development more with reference to technology component, namely from visual education to audiovisual education, the emergence of educational television, programmed instructions and teaching machines, individualized instruction, interactive instruction through computer and so on. In the process, Reiser has also drawn from the emergence of the psychological schools particularly the Behaviourist School. Swiss author Borivoj Brdicka traces its development as an inter-disciplinary subject drawing heavily from Sociology, Psychology and Philosophy. Kulkarni and Ely provided graphic presentations to indicate how educational technology has derived its inspiration and substance from different disciplines of human knowledge. However, the emphasis on technology have had a restricting effect on the authors in deriving the history within a conceptual framework that can be used to assess whether educational technology has emerged as a discipline or otherwise.

The history of educational technology—both for its conceptual evolution and development in practices have been limited by US centred developments. For an authentic history of educational technology it would be interesting to review the philosophies and practices of education that flourished in these countries. Here is an effort to trace, from Indian scriptures, some of the seeds of modern concepts of education in general and educational technology in particular.

Education is all about human development. Hence, first step is to appreciate the nature of human beings. The Indian scriptures richly depict human beings in terms of structures and evolution of consciousness. The *Katha Upanishad* takes a comprehensive view in the Parable of the Chariot:

Atmanam rathinam viddhi, sariram ratham eva tu:

Buddhim tu saradhim viddhi, man ah pragraham eva ca.

Indriyani hayam ahur visayam tesu gocaran
Atmendriya-mano-yuktambhoktety ahur manisinah.

(Katha Upanishad, 1.3.3 Transliteration into English by S. Radhakrisnan 1998)

"Know the self as the Lord of the Chariot and the body as verily, the chariot, know intellect as the charioteer and the mind as verily, the reins.

The senses, they say, are the horses; the object of the sense the paths (they range over); (the self) associated with the body, the senses and the mind—wise men declare is the enjoyer". (English rendering by S. Radhakrisnan, 1998).

The subsequent *slokas* in the parable emphasize on the ability and efficiency of the mind to control the senses that either lead to destination and goals, or dissipate the total energy. Education is training the senses (horses) to be receptive and sensitive, mind to control the senses, intelligence to be discriminative to give right direction, and body to be able to host the self—the one that is part of the Total Consciousness. The business of education covers all these dimensions.

Swami Vivekananda described 'manifestation of the perfection already in man' as the purpose of education. The focus, here, is 'perfection already in man'; again holistic. The report of the International Commission on Education for the 21st Century contributes to the same contention as it designates 'Learning to Be' (not learning to become) as one of the four pillars of learning (UNESCO, 1996). The contemporary definition of educational technology is optimizing human learning as a means to the end of manifestation of the perfection.

In Indian literature, knowledge (*Vidya*) has been classified into two categories: *paravidya* and *aparavidya*. *Paravidya* is the direct knowledge through experience and perception (often extra-sensory) achieved through *sadhana*. *Aparavidya* is the indirect knowledge or *paroksha gyan* achieved through secondary sources often through sensory mechanism. The classification later found expression in Bertrand Russell when he classified knowledge as derived through 'descendence' and 'acquaintance'. What we learn in schools and colleges are classified as *aparavidya* or *paroksha gyan*. But, how does learning happen?

Sikshavalli in the *Taitteriya*, depicts the process of education as:

> "Acarya purva-rupam, antevasy uttara-rupam, vidya sandhi, pravachanas samdhanam, ity adhividyam". (Taitteriya Upanishad, 1.4.1)

"The teacher is the prior form; the pupil is the later form, knowledge is their junction; instruction is the connection" (Radhakrisnan, 1998). Importantly, it does not accept the contemporary view of transfer of knowledge from the teacher to the student as education. Instruction is the connection, and knowledge is the junction. In effect, it discards the behaviourist model of instructive learning in favour of cognitivist theory of constructivist learning. This view gets further strengthened in

> *"Saha Nababatu, Saha Nau Bhunaktu saha birya karababahai Tejaswinavadhitamavastu ma vidwisabahai".*

(He, the supreme God, may protect us both (The teacher and the pupil), may nourish us both, may we both perform the heroic deeds together. May our study be for sharpening our minds. May we not envy each other, may we always live together happily.)

This professes learning together and growing together—the fundamentals of contemporary concept of learning organizations. It emphasizes on the importance of continuity of learning.

On the issue of method of learning with quality, two important formulations are worth quoting. One approach talks of four stages to quality learning:

1. Listen to the teacher
2. Study
3. Teach
4. Apply.

The four-stage learning indicates: firstly, that any one source is not enough; secondly, it offers a taxonomy of learning—moving from listening to application for transcending from lower to higher level of cognition, that reminds modern day taxonomies of Bloom, Briggs, Merrill and others.

The second is a multi-channel learning paradigm professed in the *Hastana Satak* of the great epic *Mahabharata*:

Acaryat Padamadatte
Padam sishya swa-medhaya
Padamekam swa brahmachirivvi,
Padam kala kramena hi.

A quarter of the learning accrues from the teacher, one quarter from self-study and talent, one quarter is derived from interaction with peers, and the rest with time *through experience* (emphasis added by author). Once again, quality in education is to be achieved through multi-channel learning which found articulation in 1994 with the formation of IMAGE (International Multi-channel Learning in Education).

Similarly, interactivity as a means of learning has been emphasized in *Bhagwat Gita 'pranipatena pariprasnena sevaya'* (learning happens through respectful enquiries with the Guru and depicted in *Yagyabalka-Maitreyee Sambad*, dialogue between Yama and Nachiketa in the *Upanishads*. Modern pedagogy emphasizes on interactive learning for higher order cognition.

In the Gurukulas, depending upon the propensities of the student, there was a separate curriculum for each learner (Differentiated Instructional Design—Mukhopadhyay and Parhar 2001). For example, same Guru Dronacharya taught specialized archery to Arjuna but *gada* to Bhima and Duryodhana. The learning was considred complete only when a disciple performed at the level of mastery (Mastery Learning).

Assessment of learning outcome was comprehensive—knowledge, skills, attitudes and such other higher human values. There were predefined indicators: *Sa vidya ya vimuktaye* (that is education which liberates—liberates from the bondage of *agyan* and *avidya*). Thus, only when one is liberated can he/

she be called educated. Another, *vidya dadati vinayam* (education inculcates modesty) and that enables one to differentiate between *paravidya* and *aparavidya* (or *avidya*). Thus, one who is characterized by 'humility of learning' rather than by 'arrogance of knowledge' can be considered duly educated.

For greater details, readers are well advised to consult more specialized books like: *The Educational System of the Ancient Indian Hindus* by Santosh K. Das, and *Ancient Indian Education* by R.K. Mookherjee.

There is, however, a disconnection between the rich ancient Indian wisdom and modern Indian educational system largely due to the dismantling of traditional educational institutions during the nine centuries of Muslim and British rule, particularly the latter one. The Charter Act of 1813 and Macaulay's Minute of 1835 dealt body-blows to such Indian educational traditions.

Educational Technology: Contributing Disciplines

The first and the foremost component of the conceptual framework is a source of substance and inspiration of the subject. Ely contends that educational technology has hardly anything of its own; it has primarily managed its appearance by joining significantly from other disciplines (table 1).

Kulkarni (1986) also provided a graphic presentation of various disciplines that contributed to the growth and development of educational technology. Brdicka dealt with this issue in great details. We may not hence need to deal with it here once again. It should suffice to acknowledge that educational technology draws its conceptual contents from various social and behavioural sciences and its applied technology component from various disciplines of science and technology.

Evolution of Conceptual Contents

My predecessors on the subject have traced the history of educational technology around three major landmarks:

Table 1: Development Sequence and Scientific Areas that Contribute to Educational Technology

Development Sequence	*Behavioural Sciences*	*Management Sciences*	*Physical Sciences*
Principles	Learning Perception Cognition Motivation Measurement	Systems Approach Management Cybernetics Macroeconomics Microeconomics	Optics Mechanics Electricity Circuits Chemistry
Techniques based on scientific principles	Programmed learning Learners Analysis Task Analysis Reinforcement Scheduling Message Design Test Construction	Needs Assessment Systems Analysis Systems Design Cost Effectiveness analysis	Optical Engineering Communications Engineering Chemical Engineering Electrical Engineering
Artifacts produced by applying scientific principles	Learning materials and activities that satisfy the conditions of learning	Management by objectives Systematically designed learning systems	Devices for transmitting, e.g., television, radio, telephone Devices for storing and Retrieving e.g., computers

Source: Stakenas R.G., Kaufman R. 1981, Technology in Education: Its Human Potential, *Phi Delta Kappa*.

- Visual instruction and audiovisual instruction
- Systems approach
- Individualized instruction

An alternative framework can evolve by considering conceptual developments like systems approach, instructional design and developments in application of educational technology namely, instructional methods and techniques like classroom instruction, individualized instruction, audio-visual instruction.

Systems Approach

One of the major developments that shaped the growth of instructional and educational technology is the systems approach. As mentioned earlier, that ancient Indian education as evident from scriptures linked educational goals, choice of content of learning, adopted multi-channel instruction including individualized instruction and a comprehensive method of evaluation indicates a holistic, rather systems approach to education. There have been several definitions and efforts to define systems approach. Banathy (1968) defined it "as a self-correcting, logical process for the planning, development and implementation of instruction….. According to him it provides a procedural framework to analyze and find the best way to achieve, to identify the components that are most suitable to the successful performance of the system, and finally continuous evaluation of the system. The development of the systems approach to design the instruction have been contributed by several scholars. The concern for systems approach in education originated from the need to give an empirical basis to the design and improvement of instruction (Reiser, 1987). Johann Herbert, in the mid 1800s called upon scientific research to be the basis for guiding instructional practice. This was carried forward by several scholars at a later stage by Joseph Mayer Rice, and later by Edward L. Thorndike who "established empirical investigation as the basis for a science of instruction… he was the exemplar of what might be done by empirical theorizing and investigation (Saetller, 1968). The interest in empirical methods to solve problems became more and more popular leading to task analysis and object specification which form the basis for the later development of programmed learning.

The emergence of programmed instruction is associated with B.F. Skinner. Heinich (1970) indicated that "programmed instruction has been credited by some with introducing the systems approach to education. By analyzing and breaking down content into specific behavioural objectives, devising the necessary steps to achieve the objectives, setting up procedures to try out and revise the steps, and by validating the programme against attainment of the objectives, programmed instruction succeeded in creating a small but effective self instructional system—a technology of instruction". The concept of task analysis in programmed instruction was further expanded by Gagne who indicated the hierarchical relationships between tasks and sub tasks; he insisted that super-ordinate tasks must be built upon subordinate tasks. This will lead to the concept of interdependability. The second important component emerging out of the programmed learning movement is the specifications of behavioural objectives. Tyler wrote in 1934, "each objective must be defined in terms which clarify the kind of behaviour which the course should help to develop". The most significant contribution that was brought in to give a boost to this concept of the behavioural objectives is by Benjamin Bloom (Taxonomy of Educational Objectives, 1956). However, the movement had to wait till early 60s and take a new impetus from Robert Mager's book, "*Preparing Objectives for Programmed Instruction*" in 1962. Subsequently, several others like Gagne, Anderson, Merrill, Briggs, and others came up with alternative taxonomies.

The systems approach movement also brought in along with the instructional technology the issues of evaluation like criteria referenced testing, formative evaluation, summative evaluation and other related concepts.

Instructional Design

The most important contribution of the systems approach to education is the development of Instructional Design. The statement, "whereas physicians engineer health, and architects engineer space, instructional designers engineer human performance." (Van Patten, 1989) succinctly focus on the role and critical importance of instructional design.

There is a wide divergence of views among the researchers regarding the relative contribution of various schools of Psychology. One contention is that instructional design has grown out of the systems approach with its roots firmly in behaviourist psychology, that has dominated instructional design for the past three decades (Strain, 1994). The other school of thought claims that instructional design developed in the 1980s by Gagne, Merrill, Reigeluth and Scandura is largely due to the cognitive learning theories (Hannafin and Reiber, 1989). More recent developments are due to constructivist learning theories. The development in the post 1990s indicates an eclectic approach—the emphasis is no longer on any one theory. Instructional designers draw upon and incorporate from different learning theories. Thus, instructional design is seen as a part of a larger design science, in which the designer borrows scientific principles from various theories, mixes those with other information and applies the results to meet human needs (Van Patten, 1989). David Merrill changed his own contention of Component Display Theory (CDT) according to Merrill and Twitchwell (1994), to introduce Instructional Transaction Theory (Merrill, 1999) as he did not find CDT good enough for expert computer modelling in instructional design.

The dual attraction of meeting the human needs and designing instruction led to considerable new experiments on instruction—programmed instruction (PI), personalized system of instruction (PSI), and teaching and teacher classroom behaviour. Whereas PI, PSI and other interactive instructional methods remained peripheral innovations, researches on teaching and teacher behaviour targeted at the core classroom process, that were the most dominant instructional events in schools and colleges. The basic agenda of these researches were to assess the impact of teacher classroom behaviour on student learning; and design instruction (which, later, came to be known as instructional strategy) in a manner that optimizes learning of the majority of students. Works of Ned A. Flanders (1970), Net L. Gage (1979) and a few others significantly influenced the conceptual and methodological aspects of such researches.

The Indian researchers picked up the thread as teacher, and teacher classroom behaviour was identified as an area of planned research in the Center of Advanced Study in Education, at M.S. University of Baroda. A comprehensive review of such studies completed in 1970s onwards have been reviewed by

Jangira and Sharma (1974), Passi and Sansanwal (1991), and Singh (1997). Most of these studies centered around, directly or indirectly, on instructional design resulting in programmed teaching. Instructional design also featured sharply in the research and development activities in PI, PSI, group interactive learning, mastery learning, media based learning, etc.

As the mode and method of learning undergoes paradigm shifts due to various new learning resources and new understanding of human cognition and affective processes, instructional designers are continuously challenged to update their repertoire of designs. Classrooms are no more the monopoly of knowledge and wisdom. There have been dramatic developments in, and diversification of, sources of knowledge; and, a quantum jump in the power of the new sources like television, radio, computer and the other forms of knowledge networks. New instructional designs have been constructed to usher in the benefits of a multi-channel learning systems (Mukhopadhyay and Parhar 2001). Instructional design which is considered a component of educational technology itself has emerged as a subject of independent study at Simon Frazier, Syracuse University, and other institutions.

Classroom Instruction

Classroom based teaching-learning process is the most common among the various instructional techniques and strategies. Also, it poses the longest tradition ever anywhere in the world. Thousands of years ago, ancient Indian education as well as other similar educational systems provided instruction to students through classroom based processes. The nature and the composition of classroom however underwent dramatic changes in the post Industrial Revolution. In fact, the board of classroom based processes can itself be described as a mechanism of mass production system compared to the Gurukula traditions of India where few students used to learn from the guru. Because of its widespread application it is not surprising that classroom instruction has attracted major attention of the researchers in the contemporary period.

The classical Herbartian steps that are used in planning the lessons for the new teacher trainees is particularly an effort to structure classroom processes. Of course, the focus is on the teacher and his/her presentation. The verbal communication of the teacher takes the centre-stage in classroom based processes. It is probably in this context that teaching has been classified as an art *vs.* science. When teaching is an art, the teacher offered is an accident; whereas when teaching is a science many individuals with average communications skill can be developed as a teacher (Greer, 2003). One of the early efforts in understanding the classroom processes and structure was the initiative by Ned A. Flanders (1962) who developed Interactive Analyses Category System that could measure and quantify classroom interaction between student and teacher. Although classrooms are seen more as place for cognitive transactions, the large-scale research indicated the effective component of the classroom processes. At a later stage, similar efforts have been undertaken by other researchers to ascertain the cognitive processes and transaction in classrooms. As mentioned earlier, similar researches were done in India at the Centre of Advanced Study in Education in Baroda that generated massive data and information on status and styles of Indian classrooms. There are new endeavours to facilitate learning through continuous measurement for assessing the entry behaviour and continuously monitoring learning.

Individualized Instruction

Another important movement in the history of instructional technology is individualized instruction. It can be traced back to ancient Indian Gurukula tradition of learning that flourished more than 5,000 years ago; to mid 1800s and as well as in the Greek and Roman era where pupils were taught individually by the tutors. Till the middle of 1800s, individualized instruction was seen as a common frame where children of different ages make it to one teacher in a one-room school house. (Grittner 1975 and Kulik 1982). This system of instruction marginally changed with adoption of monitorial system developed by Josef

Lancaster and Andrew Bell. It was during that time that the graded schools were brought in and group instruction became the new order. Nonetheless, there are several efforts and major schools that contributed to the individualized instruction. Frederick Burk developed individual systems in 1912-13 for use in the elementary schools at San Francisco. It is at later stage that Burk's staff developed the Winnetka Plan. It was developed by Carleton Washburne in 1919. Helen Parkhurst simultaneously developed the Dalton plan which were first implemented in a school for the disabled children in Dalton, Massachusetts.

The initial enthusiasm and interest in individualized approaches such as the Winnetka plan and Dalton plan waned, though individualized approaches significantly influenced the thoughts and practices of education. The major contribution was the idea that learners can demonstrate mastery in a set of skills; in fact it should be preferred that before moving to the next skill he/she demonstrates the mastery of the skill.

The most important movement in the individualized instruction is programmed instruction that began in 1954 with the publication of B.F. Skinner's article "The Science of Learning And the Art of Teaching". There have been several contributions to programmed instruction and advanced programming. The basic feature was that a learning material could be spelt out into small steps based on task analysis and content analysis. The learner is expected to learn one step at a time; he or she is immediately tested and given the feedback. This sequential step allows the learner to learn and achieve mastery over one step before moving to the others. There have been major experiments on different types of programming like linear and branching as well as on different types of frames like small and large frame.

E.D.L. Thorndike and Sydney L. Pressey are considered as the forerunners of programmed instruction movement. As early as 1925, Pressey demonstrated the teaching machine in the American Psychological Association. Several innovative features were added to the teaching machine during the 1920s and early 30s. However, Pressey discontinued his work in this area (Pressey 1964). The teaching machine got a new impetus almost after 30 years with Skinner's work on Programmed Instruction. Large number of programmes are written for use in the schools, in the army, in business and industry. Many private companies also responded to this new movement. A journal devoted exclusively to the topic of programmed instruction was originated; numerous books and articles were written. The programmed instruction movement entered India in the mid 60s; very similar applications are found in India as well when programmed materials are developed for schools, industry particularly banking and life insurance corporation. Indian Association of Programmed Learning was formed in 1969 and it brought out a Journal dedicated to the subject, *"Indian Journal of Programmed Learning"*.

In the late 60s, emerged the Personalized System of Instruction (PSI), more popularly known as Keller Plan. This is an instructional approach that allows students to proceed in an instructional sequence at his or her own pace but achieve mastery; wherever necessary students can be used as proctors. Keller (1968, 1974) identified five features of the personalized system of instruction which are different from conventional instructional methods. These are: the unit mastery requirement, use of student self pacing, the use of student proctors, reliance on written instruction and de-emphasis on lectures. Several Indian scholars took serious interest in Keller plan and conducted experiments. However, unlike programmed instruction, personalized system of instruction did not catch the same level of imagination with the Indian scholars.

Both programmed instruction as well as the personalised system of instruction emphasized on achieving the highest possible level of performance by tying the time and mode of learning. The seeds of mastery learning was steadily being sown. However, the actual credit goes to Benjamin Bloom and his students at the University of Chicago. The major difference was in the approach to the mastery learning. The Keller plan emphasized on mastery, yet it was teacher paced instruction. In mastery learning, initially the teacher presents the instruction using conventional group based teaching methods but subsequently the activities are transferred to the students for small group study, peer tutoring and individual review of alternative instructional materials such as textbooks, work groups and non-print material. Thus, steadily the mastery learning brought in along with the instructive processes some dimensions of constructive learning. Interestingly, in the Indian Gurukula system, where individualized instruction was to the extent that the Guru constructed a curriculum for each student and set the standards, unless a student performed at that specified level of mastery, learning was not considered complete and the student could not graduate (see Das, 1930). Thus Gurukula system practised mastery learning.

There are several other programmes of individualised instruction like audio tutorial approach, individually prescribed instruction (IPI), programme for learning in accordance with needs (PLAN), individually guided education (IGE), etc. The interest in individualized instructional systems like these faded fairly fast. The attention turned towards use of computer technology, particularly microcomputers in presenting individualized instruction. Due to the interactive capabilities, computers can be programmed to adapt instruction to the individual needs. Initially computers were used in education and training. In 1950s, much of the early works in CAI was done at IBM. During the 1960s, there were several major efforts in various universities to undertake research in collaboration with computer organisations and to see the effect of CAI on student learning. During the 1970s, the movement continued to grow. There has been tremendous growth in the use of microcomputers in the schools in the 1980s.

Audiovisual Instruction

It can be traced back to 17th century with the work of Johann Comenius who emphasized primarily on the sense organs as the basic channel for learning in his book, *Orbis Sensualium Pictus* (The Visible World in Pictures) in 1650. Next influence was by Johann Pestalozzi in 1800s. The actual audiovisual movement picked up in the 20th century with the opening of the school museums in various states in the United States. In 1913, Thomas Edison proclaimed: "books will soon be obsolete in schools. It is possible to teach every branch of human knowledge with the motion picture. Our school system will be completely changed in the next ten years" (cited in Saetller, 1968). Although Thomas Edison prediction did not come true, audiovisual movement kept growing during the remainder of the decade, 1920s and through the 1930s. However, certain advances in technology impacted on the quality of films and slides; radio broadcasting expanded, sound recording and motion pictures with sound became reality, and fostered the growth of visual instruction; indeed it changed to audiovisual instruction. Despite the growth in the audiovisual instruction, the educational community did not seem to be greatly affected (McCluskey 1981). According to many students of history of educational technology, a number of textbooks on the topic of visual instruction appeared. Reiser (1987) refers to *Visualising the Curriculum* by Charles F. Hoban, Sr., Charles F. Hoban Jr. and Stanley B. Zissman in 1937 as a landmark. It was during this time that the authors conceptualised and presented a hierarchy of media which was further developed and elaborated by Edgar Dale in his famous book, "Cone of Experience". The main pedagogical thrust is that the audiovisual materials have the ability to present concepts in a concrete manner.

World War II brought in a new dimension to the audiovisual movement. Audiovisual devices were used extensively in the military services and in industry. During the war years, The United States Government, through its Division of Visual Aids for War Training, produced 457 industrial training films. The government purchased 55 thousand film projectors for the military and spent one billion dollars on training through films. The effect of audiovisual training on American army is well illustrated by the German Chief of General Staff, "we had everything calculated perfectly except the speed with which America was able to train its people. Our major miscalculation was in underestimating their quick and complete mastery of film education (Reiser, 1987)". This experience of the army in training people with diverse backgrounds kindled new interest in the visual instruction in education. It led to a whole range of research in audiovisual education.

The most significant development in audiovisual instructional movement is the emergence of television as a medium of delivering instruction. Before 1950 there have been several efforts in garnering television for instructional purposes. The actual movement, however, started in the post 1950s. The factor that actually spurred the growth of educational television was the decision by Federal Communication Commission in 1952 to set aside as many as 242 television channels for educational purposes. By 1955, there were 17 such stations in United States and by 1960 it had grown to more than 50. As Hezel (1980) indicates: "the teaching role has been ascribed to public broadcasting since its origin. Especially prior to the 1960s, educational broadcasting was seen as a quick, efficient, inexpensive means of satisfying the nations, instructional needs". However, the enthusiasm of instructional television waned by mid 60s partly due to mediocre quality of the programmes produced; many of them were just around presenting a teacher delivering a lecture. Although the educational television lost its glory but it continued to be present and used in many school systems. Some large-scale projects such as the Sesame Street television series received favourable publicity with many instructors.

Beginning of Indian educational television in 1962 is linked to the problem of quality of science education and shortage of science teachers. But the landmark was the SITE (Satellite Instructional Television in Education) in early 1970s. The National Policy on Education 1986, for the first time, looked at educational technology as an item for policy formulation. There was a specific recommendation about extended use of educational technology primarily comprising educational radio, educational television, and computer literacy programmes in schools. State Institutes of Educational Technology were established in several Indian provinces to develop broadcast software for educational radio and television. Educational television spread far and wide in Indian higher education; Audiovisual Resource Centres and Educational Media Resource Centre was established forming the Consortium of Educational Communication (CEC).

The latest initiative is the launching of a dedicated satellite for education by the middle of 2004 to support broadcast radio and television, interactive radio and television, interactive computer communication, video conferencing through 72 channels supporting not only education at all levels of the formal system, but also including education of the women, youth, toddlers, senior citizens, employees, etc. (for details, see, *Educating the Nation: Need for a Dedicated Satellite* by Marmar Mukhopadhyay, 2002).

Meanwhile, change in the conceptual processes and thinking was steadily emerging. James Finn, then President of Department of Audiovisual Instruction established a Commission on Definition and Terminology whose goal was to define the field and the terminology associated with it (Ely, 1983). The changed contention of audiovisual instruction was on the design and use of messages that control the learning processes rather than with audiovisual devices that traditionally had been the focus of the field. However, many of the practitioners continued to focus their attention on audiovisual devices. According to Lumsdaine (1964), in one sense, instructional technology referred to the use of equipment for presenting instructional materials; in a second sense, instructional technology could be thought of as the application of scientific, particularly theories of learning in order to improve instruction.

Simultaneously there was a steady development of the new school of thought promoting interactivity as the toll for constructing learning. There are several examples of interactive learning in the Gurukula tradition, Blomm's Mastery Learning, etc. where the onus of learning is on the learner. Indeed, the hallmark of constructive processes of learning is the interactive learning. There are several forms of interactive learning.

Deriving the lessons from the interactive learning, and

the emergence of computer technology, interaction could be predesigned by programming the computer. New developments in information and communication technology ushered in videoconferencing, audio conferencing, interactive radio, interactive television, interactive computer communication, etc. resulting into virtual classrooms.

The Internet brought in a new era in educational delivery particularly interactive learning. With the growing technological capability, Internet is now able to carry data, information, pictures, visuals, animations, etc. It has emerged as a complete delivery system. Web-based education and e-learning are catching up all over the world though the issue of relative efficiency and cost effectiveness have not been resolved (Bates, 2002).

Conclusion

Optimizing human learning has been a concern of educators through ages through out the world. Growth and development of educational technology is the outcome of this perennial search for design, development, application and assessment of instructional systems. It had to draw its larger inspiration from studies of societies and social growth since education is socially embedded; from studies of human cognition and affection since it deals with optimization of learning of each human being. It has over a period of time generated its own vocabulary, conceptual basis in the form of systems approach and instructional design, its own tools and techniques in a variety of forms of instructional strategies. It has garnered support from science and technology to facilitate communication and transactions. Indeed, educational technology has created a world of its own without shutting its doors and windows to the developments in allied fields. At the inner core, educational technology has a sound theoretical construct with sensors in the softer outer layers to receive new messages and absorb, constantly updating itself. It is a field of study that has not ceased to grow, nor even slowed down its pace.

REFERENCES

Anzalone, S., The case for multi-channel learning, in Anzalone, S. (ed). *Multi-channel Learning: Connecting All to Education*, Washington D.C.: EDC, 1995.

Association for Educational Communication and Technology (AECT) Definition of Educational Technology, Washington D.C.: AECT, 1977.

Banathy, B.H., *Instructional systems*, Belmont, CA: Fearon. 1968.

Bates, T. *National Policies on e-Learning*, Paris: IIEP, 2002

Bloom, Benjamin, *Taxonomy of Educational Objectives: The Classification of Educational Goals, Handbook 1 Cognitive Domain*, New York: David Mckay, 1956.

Brdicka, Borivoj, *The Influence of Technology on Human Mind*, Prague: Charles University, http://it.pedf.cuni.cz/-bobr/hmind/index.htm

Das, Santosh K., The Educational System of the Ancient Indian Hindus, New Delhi: Gyan, 1986.

Ely, D.P. Field of Study, in Eraut, M. (ed), International *Encyclopedia of Education*, New York: Pergamon, 1989.

Ely, D.P., The definition of educational technology: An emerging stability *Educational Considerations*, 10(2), 1983.

Eraut, M. (ed), International Encyclopaedia of Educational Technology, New York: Pergamon, 1989.

Flanders, Ned A., *Analyzing Teaching Behaviour*, California: Addison-Wesley, 1970.

Gage, N.L., *Scientific Basis of the Art of Teaching*, New York: Teachers' College Press, 1979.

Greer, R.D., A Real Science and Technology of Education, Teachers College, Columbia University, 2003.

Grittner, F.M., Individualized instruction: An historical perspective, *Modern Language Journal*, 59, 1975.

Hannafin, M.J. and Rieber, L., Psychological Foundations of Instructional Design for Emerging Computer-based Instructional Technologies: Part I, *ETR&D*, 37(2), 1989.

Hastana Satak of the great epic *Mahabharata*:

Heinich, R., *Technology and the management of instruction* (Association for Educational Communication and Technology Monograph No. 4). Washington, DC: Association for Educational Communications and Technology, 1970.

Hezel, R.T., Public broadcasting: Can it teach ? *Journal of Communication*, 30, 1980

Jangira, N.K. and Sharma, S., Teaching and Teacher Behaviour: A Trend Report, in Buch M.B.(ed). *Survey of Research in Education*, Baroda: CASE, 1974.

Keller, F.S. and Sherman, J.G. *The Keller Plan Handbook: Essays on a Personalised System of Instruction*, California: Benjamin Menlo Park, 1974.

Keller, F.S. Good-bye teacher..., *Journal of Applied Behavioural Analysis*, 1968.

Kulik, J.A., Individualized systems of instruction. In H.E. Mitzel (Ed.), *Encyclopedia of educational research* (5th ed.). New York: Macmillan1982.

Kulkarni, S.S. *Introduction to Educational Technology*, New Delhi: Oxford & IBH, 1986.

Lumsdaine, A.A., Educational Technology, programmed learning, and instructional science. In E.R. Hilgard (Ed.) *Theories of learning and instruction: The sixty-third yearbook of the National Society for the Study of Education*, Part I. Chicago: University of Chicago Press, 1964.

Mager, Robert, *"Preparing Objectives for Programmed Instruction"* in 1962.

McCluskey, F.D., DVI, DAVI, AECT: A long view. In J.W. Brown & S.N. Brown (Eds.), *Educational media yearbook:* 1981. Littleton. CO: Libraries Unlimited 1981.

Merrill, M.D. and Twitchwell, D.G. (eds), *Instructional Design Theory*, Englewood Cliffs, NJ: Educational Technology Publications, 1994

Merrill, M.D. Instructional Transaction Theory (ITT): Instructional Design Based on Knowledge Objects, Reigeluth Charles M. (ed.), *Instructional Design Theories and Models A new paradigm of Instructional theory* Volume II, LEA Publishers, Mahwah, New Jersey, 1999

Mookherjee, R.K. *Ancient Indian Education*, New Delhi: Motilal Banarasidas, 1969

Mukhopadhyay, M., Multi-channel Learning: A case of National Open School, India, in Anzalone, S. (ed). *Multi-channel Learning: Connecting All to Education*, Washington D.C.: EDC, 1995.

Mukhopadhyay, Marmar and Parhar, Madhu, Instructional design in Multi-channel Learning Systems, *British Journal of Educational technology*, 32(5), November, 2001

Mukhopadhyay, Marmar, *Educating the Nation: Need for a Dedicated Satellite*, Ahmedabad: DECU, 2002.

Mukhopadhyay, Marmar, Educational Technology in Encyclopaedia of Indian Education, New Delhi: NCERT, (in press).

Mukopadhyay Marmar, Preface in Mukopadhyay M. et.al (eds), *Optimizing Human Learning*, Delhi: Amar Prakashan, 1993,

Passi, B.K. and Sansanwal, S., Research in Teaching, in Buch, M.B.*(ed)*, *Fourth Survey of Research in Education*, New Delhi: NCERT, 1991.

Percival, F. and Ellington, H. *A Handbook of Educational Technology*, London: Kogan Page, 1984.

Pressey, S.L., Auto instruction: Perspectives, problems, potentials. In E.R. Hilgard (Ed.) *Theories of learning and instruction: the sixty-third yearbook of the National Society for the Study of Education, Part I.* Chicago: University of Chicago Press, 1964.

Radhakrishnan, S., *The Principal Upansihads*, New Delhi: Harper Collins, 1998

Reiser, R.A., The concept and evolution of educational technology, in Gagne, R.M. (ed) *"Instructional Technology: Foundation" Foundations* Lawrence Erlbaum Associations Publishers, London, 1987.

Reiser, Robe rt A., Instructional Technology: A History in Gagne Robert M. (ed.), *Instructional Technology: Foundations* Lawrence Erlbaum Associations Publishers, London, 1987.

Saettler, P., *A history of instructional technology*. New York: McGraw-Hill 1968.

Singh, L.C. and Jaimini, N., Teaching Strategies, in NCERT, *Fifth Survey of Research in Education*, New Delhi: NCERT, 1997.

Stakenas R G, Kaufman R., Technology in Education: Its Human Potential, Phi Delta Kappa, 1981.

Strain, J., Pathways to a Profession Designing Instruction for Instructional Designers, In Parer, M.S., *Unlocking Open Learning*, Victoria: Monash University, 1994.

UNESCO, Learning: The Treasure Within, Paris: UNESCO, 1996

Van Patten, J., What is Instructional Design, in Johnson, K.A. and Foa, L.J. *Instructional Design: New Alternatives for Effective Education and Training*. New York, Macmillan, 1989.

2

Instructional Systems Design

CHARLES M. REIGELUTH and B.J. BEATTY

What is Instructional Systems Design?

"Instruction" is defined broadly as anything that intentionally facilitates human learning and development of any kind, including that which facilitates a learner's construction of knowledge—instruction subsumes construction. "Design" is a process whereby instruction is brought into being. And "systems" conveys two meanings: (1) that instruction should be viewed as a system and (2) that a systems approach should be used to design instruction. Therefore, instructional systems design is a field dedicated to helping people to do a better job of facilitating human learning and development of all kinds. To fulfill this mission, its knowledge base addresses both process and product (or means and ends) for facilitating human learning and development

The product knowledge base is concerned with what the instruction should be like as it unfolds with the learner. This is referred to as instructional design theory. The process knowledge base is concerned with how instruction should be planned and instructional resources developed prior to its occurrence with learners. It includes knowledge about such activities as analysis, design, development, implementation, and evaluation (Gagnóóe & Briggs, 1974; Dick & Carey, 1996). The process knowledge base has been described extensively elsewhere (see e.g., Gustafson & Branch, 1997) and will not be addressed here. Rather, this chapter will provide an overview of what instructional theory is and what sorts of changes it is currently undergoing.

Department of Education, Indiana University, USA.

Descriptive vs. Design Theory

Most educational research studies focus on descriptive knowledge: describing the learning process, instructional process, or outcomes that result from the use of an instructional process. Unfortunately, this kind of knowledge is not directly useful to teachers and other instructional designers, who are interested in knowing what methods of instruction to use in a particular situation. This kind of goal-oriented knowledge is called design science (Simon, 1969) or design theory (Reigeluth, 1983; 1999) and is generated through decision-oriented inquiry (Cronbach & Suppes, 1969) and formative research (Reigeluth & Frick, 1999), in which the major criterion is preferability rather than validity.

Instructional design theory offers methods of instruction that will be most likely to foster the desired learning outcomes in different situations. These methods are not 100 per cent guaranteed to result in the desired outcomes, but they have been found effective in similar situations. There are several important aspects of the instructional situation that may influence which methods will work best. One is values or philosophy about learning and instruction. Values can concern either the content (goals) or the methods (means) of instruction. If an educator designing instruction for a history course values learning community, for example, s/he is likely to choose instructional methods that draw students together to collaborate. If an educator values self-regulated learning, s/he is likely to choose methods that emphasize self-awareness, self-control, self-evaluation, and goal setting. Some instructional methods may be effective for multiple sets of values and goals, but typically a method is consistent with one particular set of values. Thus, it is important for a design theory to include a statement of the values upon which it is based.

A second important aspect of the instructional situation to consider when choosing methods is the desired outcomes. It is helpful to think in terms of two kinds of outcomes. Learning outcomes represent what is being learned, whereas instructional outcomes represent criteria for judging how good the instruction is. Regarding learning outcomes, different types of learning are often best fostered by different types of instructional methods. Therefore, learning outcomes (or goals) are an important basis for selecting methods. Instructional outcomes fall into three categories: effectiveness, efficiency, and appeal (Reigeluth & Merrill, 1979). In many cases, one method may be the most effective but not the most efficient or appealing, and so on. Therefore, the desired instructional outcomes are also important for selecting methods.

A third aspect of the instructional situation is the conditions under which a method will likely work better than other methods. Conditions are beyond the control of a teacher or instructional designer, and they may include student characteristics, content characteristics, learning environment characteristics, and instructional development constraints. For example, in web-based instruction, regular and frequent student access to specific communication technologies, such as a web-based bulletin board system, is a condition that must be met for social interaction to be an effective method (Beatty, 2002).

To summarize, instructional design theories present guidelines that indicate which instructional methods are likely to work best, considering the educator's values, the desired learning and instructional outcomes, and the conditions under which the instruction will take place. Instructional design theories provide guidance to educators on how to teach, in contrast to curriculum theory's focus on guidance about what to teach and learning theory's focus on describing how people learn (largely internal cognitive processes).

New Demands on Instructional Theory

There has been much discussion over the past few decades about the shift in paradigm from an industrial-age worldview to an information-age worldview, and the resulting impact of this shift upon education (Ackoff, 1981; Banathy, 1991; Bell, 1973; Reigeluth, 1994; Toffler, 1970, 1980, 1990). This shift also impacts Instructional Systems Design (ISD) as a field (Reigeluth

& Nelson, 1997). Paradigm shifts occur when fundamental changes arise in major characteristics of a system (Kuhn, 1996). The fundamental changes that distinguish the industrial-age and information-age paradigms of education and training include the following:

- Shift from a concern for standardization to a concern for customization
- Shift from central, bureaucratic control to autonomous, team-based management
- Shift from adversarial relationships to collaborative relationships
- Shift from autocratic decision making to shared decision making
- Shift from valuing compliance to valuing initiative
- Shift from a desire for conformity to an appreciation for diversity
- Shift from one-way communication to networked communication
- Shift from compartmentalization (or departmentalization) to integration (holism)
- Shift from product orientation to process orientation
- Shift from planned obsolescence to a concern for total quality
- Shift from teacher-centered instruction to learner-centered instruction

In our current industrial-age systems of education and training, the focus is typically on sorting students: holding time constant and thereby forcing achievement to vary, and using standardized norm-referenced tests. In an information-age system the focus is on learning: allowing learning time to vary so every student can reach mastery, using performance-based, criterion-based assessments, and having students' assume some responsibility for directing their own learning. These key characteristics of information-age instructional theories are described in more detail later in this chapter.

Given this shift in our educational and training systems, it is incumbent upon instructional design theory to offer guidance as to how to create powerful information-age, learner-centered instruction. What instructional methods should be used for this new set of values, goals, and conditions? Next, we describe several instructional theories that fit the information-age characteristics.

Promising Types of Theories

Each of the types of design theory described below has been developed as the Information Age paradigm has emerged over the past few decades. Of course, there are many more types of theories than we have room to describe here.

Self-Regulated Learning Theories

Self-regulated learning theories cultivate self-regulation skills in students to help them become more effective life-long learners (Knowles, 1990; Pintrich, 1995), and they support the use of those self-regulation skills. Self-regulation skills include determining whether or not material being studied is being understood and whether or not a particular study strategy is effective. Self-regulated learning has been defined as active, goal directed, self-control of behaviour, motivation, and cognition for academic tasks by an individual student (Pintrich, 1995).

In the classroom, instructional strategies that have been effective in teaching self-regulated skills include: encouraging students to set assessment or performance criteria and select assignments, teaching students how to recognize when they need help and then how to seek help appropriately, modeling self-regulatory skills for students, asking students to reflect on their own self-regulatory experiences and habits in an essay, and many others (see e.g., Corno & Randi, 1999). Additionally, some instructional theories include strategies to help teachers develop self-regulatory skills such as using a purposive cycle of planning, enacting and reflecting on their teaching methods.

Problem-Based Learning Theories

Problem-based learning (PBL) refers to instruction that revolves around students' engagement in solving authentic problems using a rich set of true-to-life resources, such as news articles, domain experts, and field reports. PBL has been practiced informally for a long time, but was implemented formally in educational settings only as recently as the late 1960's (Barrows, 1986). Educators are using PBL approaches in various content domains, including the fields of medicine, law and management.

Some of the key features of PBL instructional theory include the use of authentic, ill-structured problems that reflect the true complexity of the content domain, providing learning resources that the student explores in their actual (not simplified) form, allowing the student to control his or her own learning process, evaluating learning outcomes using performance assessment, and incorporating student reflections about their learning process (Savery & Duffy, 1996). A major feature of PBL is that the role of the teacher changes from a central, controlling role to one more like a coach. In a PBL environment, the teacher assists the student only when needed—prompting, probing, challenging assumptions and assertions, helping students assess their learning, and encouraging students to take control of their own learning.

Social Interaction Theories

Social constructivist learning can be defined as learning that occurs as students create (construct) understandings of their world through interaction with others, such as fellow learners and experts (Bonk & Cunningham, 1998; Cobb, 1994; Duffy & Cunningham, 1996). Social constructivist values and related learning goals and characteristics include: meaningful learning, collaborative problem solving, relevance to the student, multiple perspectives, collaborative reflection, self-regulation, and learning communities or communities of practice (Lave & Wenger, 1991).

In *socio-cultural learning,* students engage in learning activities that address the social, cultural, and historical contexts of the students' environment (Vygotsky, 1978). Learning is understood to be an inherently social process but takes place within a learner's "zone of proximal development," the conceptual region just beyond an individual's capability to perform (or think) without external support of some kind. In order to operate in this zone, interaction with an external agent, such as a teacher, more capable peer, or expert, is prescribed. Some of the common aspects of socio-cultural-based instructional theory include guidance for student-centeredness, peer collaboration, the use of scaffolding, teacher-student and student-student dialogue, and consideration of the socio-historical context in the learning environment.

Simulation Theories

Simulation, or virtual world, is an effective instructional strategy to use when a "real" environment is not available for the educational experience, or when time or expense can be considerably reduced. Simulations may be highly complex, relying on high-powered technology-based systems to simulate the flight deck of an aircraft, for example. Simulations may also be simple and "low-tech," such as a paper-based activity simulating an economic exchange. Simulations provide a safe place for learning where mistakes can be used as "learning moments." Students are able to review, reflect, and try again. Using simulations, educators put students into appropriately constructed situations having features that are authentic in key ways, enabling contextualized and effective learning.

Instruction for Effect

For too long, the ISD field and educators in general have ignored learners' needs that were not directly related to cognitive outcomes. A growing realization that learners suffer if they do not undergo more than cognitive development (Goleman, 1995), and that the educational program should overtly teach other aspects of human development, have led to increased support for, and interest in, instructional theories for teaching in the *affective domain*, focusing on subjects such as emotional intelligence, attitude formation, morality, self-concept, personality development, spiritual development, feelings, and motivation, in formal and informal learning environments (Beane, 1990; Martin & Reigeluth, 1999).

Design theories have been developed to offer guidance on how to teach such affective topics more effectively. For example, one instructional program, focused on a child's social, ethical, and intellectual development, implements instructional strategies such as using classic literature that is rich in social and ethical themes to teach reading, using cooperative learning groups to develop social skills and ethical values, and using problem-solving approaches to solve disciplinary problems in school (Lewis, Watson & Schaps, 1999). This theory integrates affective instruction particularly well, since it addresses three major components at once (social, ethical, and intellectual).

Universal Principles of Instruction

Are there universal principles of instruction that should be followed no matter what the specific instructional context is? Reigeluth and Nelson (1997) described commonly-used "basic methods" of instruction, which are scientifically proven instructional strategies and tactics that have been used successfully in many different instructional theories. These basic methods, however, vary from one type of learning to another. For example, to teach all but the simplest skills, "tell, show, and do" (generality, demonstration, and practice with feedback) are basic methods that enhance the quality of instruction.

In recent years, Merrill (2000) has outlined what he calls "first principles of instruction" that he proposes universally enhance the effectiveness of all instruction. They include:

- *Problem-centered*—Learners should be engaged in solving real problems.
- *Activation of prior experience*—Relevant prior knowledge should be activated.

- *Demonstration*—New knowledge should be demonstrated to the learner.
- *Application*—New knowledge should be applied by the learner.
- *Integration*—New knowledge should be integrated into the learner's world.

Such foundational principles are very general and do not provide detailed guidance to a designer or teacher, and they should likely be implemented in vastly different ways for different situations. Nevertheless, the possibility of their existence for *all* effective instruction is exciting.

Implementing ISD: Limitations and Opportunities

Instructional theory has been implemented in many settings to meet the needs of both education and training providers. However, there are many settings that do not effectively utilize instructional theory. In this section we describe some of the reasons for this underutilization and some of the encouraging leverage points that instructional theory provides that may lead to improvements in instruction in the future.

Systemic Problems and Incompatibilities

Instructional programs in education and training are systems within a larger system, such as a corporation, school, or other institution. Also, the instructional system interacts on a peer level with other systems within the larger system. If changes in one system are not coordinated with changes in related systems, incompatibilities and systemic conflicts are inevitable. For example, if an academic department in a school decides to implement a new instructional program that involves using Internet-based resources through the school network, but doesn't coordinate with the information technology department to determine the effect on the rest of the school network, overload may result, causing network degradation for them and other users.

Systemic problems may occur due to differences in philosophical beliefs among stakeholder groups, also. For example, in some schools authentic, portfolio assessment was implemented to replace the traditional A-B-C-D-F grading system. The students and parents were provided with an extensive, written assessment that highlighted each student's strengths and weaknesses, with recommendations for follow-on studies. In some of these schools the parents reacted negatively. Many parents wanted to know their student's class rank more than they wanted a meaningful assessment of his or her performance and needs. As a result, some schools have switched back to the old way of evaluating students.

Obstacles to Implementation

Besides systemic issues, there are many other obstacles to the adoption of ISD theories. Two that we will expound upon here are teacher training and interest, and student assessment systems.

One significant obstacle to the implementation of new instructional design theories is the lack of sufficient *teacher training* and sometimes a lack of significant teacher interest. New instructional theories are often developed as part of a research program at a university or other research institution. Rarely does the funding include widespread programs to train teachers in the field how to implement the instructional theory. New and promising design theories are developed, published, possibly debated in the ISD community, and then (too often) ignored by the key implementation stakeholder, the teacher. Other times a new instructional program is given to teachers and trainers to implement, but the teacher or trainer decides to use only part of the program, or decides to use pieces of several different (and possibly incompatible) programs.

Another obstacle to significant change in instructional systems is the assessment system. In education, for example, traditional assessment systems include letter or numerical grades, advancement to the next level based upon age and "seat time" rather than learning, and a concern more for sorting students than for assessing true learning needs and progress. In training, there has traditionally been an overemphasis on counting attendance and positive trainee reviews as the key indicators of training quality. In each of these settings, this reliance on traditional, industrial-age methods of assessment tends to block the adoption of instructional methods and systems more attuned to the learning-focused paradigm.

Leverage Points and Catalysts

Even though there are many obstacles to change, there are also opportunities for change. Next, we will discuss several leverage points and catalysts that may be used to facilitate the changes needed to advance the use of instructional theories. They include technology-enabled or enhanced instruction and new assessment systems.

Technology-Enabled or Enhanced Instruction

One of the major leverage points is the use of advanced technology to enable learning-focused instructional theories. Two areas of technology-based instruction that we will address here are Computer Supported Collaborative Learning (CSCL) and online (Internet-based) systems.

CSCL Systems

CSCL systems are designed to enable collaborative learning among students through the use of computer-based systems for communication, sharing files and common workplaces, and other group collaborative efforts (Koschmann, 1996). CSCL systems have been used in many different educational settings, including school-based computer labs, computer-equipped classrooms, educational field trips, museums and other informal educational sites, and distance education programs.

One example of a CSCL system that enables new instructional methods is a system that connects students from various countries and different schools in a common project (Siegel & Kirkley, 1998). In this project, each participating class sent environmental data to all the other classes, and each class plotted worldwide climate trends. Computer-mediated communication systems facilitated rapid communication among students and scientists from around the world. New technologies such as these (computer support for communication and file sharing) are accentuating the need for new types of instruction.

Online Systems

Online systems not only support CSCL applications, but enable other new kinds of instruction as well. One significant leverage point is the ability of an online system to provide anytime, anywhere access to instruction that has been customized to meet the particular needs of each student, including those of collaboration and social interaction.

For example, consider an online system designed to provide instruction in sales techniques for a worldwide corporate training audience. A well-designed online system can evaluate the specific training needs of individual students and send them personalized, individualized instruction (such as web pages) when and where they choose to learn. An online instructional system like this enables and promotes several learner-centered aspects of the new paradigm of instruction: individualization, self-pacing, and flexible (and responsive) access.

New Assessment Systems

In most educational systems, the student assessment subsystem is an obstacle to new instructional methods, as discussed previously in this chapter. However, a different kind of assessment system could be a powerful catalyst to foster information-age instructional methods. The assessment system is key because it tends to drive the entire instructional (or learning) process. If it is a performance-based, untimed, criterion-referenced test, teachers would use learning-focused instructional methods to help students to acquire new skills and understandings. Students would continue to work on mastering a criterion until they reach the pre-established standard, so that they would be successful even if they learn at a slower rate. Clearly, assessment systems have an important influence on instruction.

Catalysts like these can help spur the use of instructional theory for crafting truly learner-centered instruction to meet the needs of information-age learners.

Design Theory-Easier to Use

Instructional design theory is easier to use than descriptive learning theory, since design theory provides guidance on what methods of instruction to use when, rather than describing how learning happens. While descriptive theory is useful in creating design theory, it is often very difficult to determine how to teach according to a particular learning theory, without an accompanying design theory based on the learning theory. Design theory provides the practical link between theories about learning and educational (or instructional) practice. For example, a learning theory such as schema theory explains how new knowledge is built into schemata through such processes as accommodation, tuning, and restructuring (Norman, 1976). An accompanying design theory, however, will include specific instructional methods that are most useful for stimulating those processes, such as providing an "advance organizer" (Ausubel, 1968) or activating a meaningful learning set (Mayer, 1979).

Into the Future

Accelerating and Deepening

We expect the paradigm shift described earlier to continue, accelerating and deepening as changes affect all aspects of life. Contributing to this shift will be advances in the power of technology, increased access to technology and services, better understanding of how to use technology effectively in education and training, and new ways of both instructing and designing instruction based on the learning-focused instructional theories discussed previously. The key markers described earlier lead us to believe that several areas of research and practice are likely to have a particularly important influence on the development of future instructional theories: virtual reality, ubiquitous computing, Web-based instruction, learning and knowledge objects, multi-channel learning, and knowledge management.

Virtual Reality

Virtual reality (VR) instructional systems use high performance computers and newly designed interfaces to provide virtual—as opposed to actual—experiences to learners. VR systems commonly use wearable computers and displays in their attempts to immerse the leaner in an experience as close to actual as possible. The goal is for the learner to suspend his or her disbelief and interact with the instructional environment as if it were real. Potential instructional applications for VR include those similar to simulations: where the "real" learning experience is not readily available due to access, expense, safety, time requirements, or some other constraints (e.g., exploring the interior of a glacier). Since many applications of VR rely upon powerful and complex computing systems, we expect that VR systems will become more prevalent in instruction as computer technologies advance and become less expensive. As powerful VR systems become available, more instructional methods for making best use of them will surely be developed.

Ubiquitous Computing

Ubiquitous computing refers to computing applications that are so common that they seem to be everywhere, part of the general landscape of life. These applications may be embedded in larger systems, often performing their functions without being noticed at all, as in our cars, for example, and our TV sets. In schools, computers were once relegated to computer labs and the library. Now, computers are in classrooms, homes, libraries, museums, backpacks, and even shirt pockets. And coupled with telecommunications and the Internet, those computers increasingly allow access to instruction any time and any place. This is placing new demands on instructional theory, particularly in the form of "on-demand" and "just-in-time" instruction (see discussion below).

Web-Based Instruction

Web-based instruction has emerged over the past decade as one of the most important developments in instructional technology. Learning "online" will continue to become more common, both in formal instructional settings and informal learning environments. Since the early 1990s, the capabilities of the web have evolved from simple presentation of information to dynamic, interactive, multimedia presentations and rich learning environments that facilitate social interaction and enable collaboration (Khan, 1997). To take advantage of these expanding capabilities, instructional theory must develop guidance on ever better ways of teaching and learning that focus on collaboration, social interaction, and multiple experiences with content to reshape the learning experience (Bates, 2001).

Learning Objects

A recent development in education and training places an emphasis on creating reusable "learning" objects (RLOs, or sometimes just "learning objects") and building instruction by combining RLOs in different ways to meet one's instructional objectives (see e.g., Wiley, 2001). Usually, each RLO is designed to "teach" one complete learning objective and includes instructional media (text, graphics, animations, etc.), practice, feedback, and assessment as needed. The Advanced Distributed Learning (ADL) initiative, sponsored by the United States government, is coordinating a major effort to standardize the creation and technical labeling of learning objects so that each is reusable in as many specific contexts as possible (ADL, 2001). The ADL initiative has created the technological foundation that will enable the widespread reuse of RLOs, but there has been little emphasis on how best to design instruction using them. This is a major challenge for instructional theory and research.

Multi-Channel Learning

Multi-channel learning involves the use of multiple channels of instruction, such as formal school, after-school tutorial programs, parent-assisted homework, audio or video lessons on tape, and distance learning media. The goal of multi-channel systems is to provide the most effective mix of instructional channels to each learner (Mukhopadhyay & Parhar, 2001). Some forms of multi-channel learning have been practiced for a long time in many cultures around the world, but formal recognition of multi-channel learning as a legitimate "educational program" option began only in the early 1990's. This approach has been very effective in several large educational programs, including the INNOTECH program in the Philippines and the OLSET program in South Africa (Anzalone, Sutaria, Desroches & Visser, 1995). This is an important approach for instructional theory to address.

Knowledge Management

Knowledge management is an emerging field concerned with the management of knowledge in an organization, especially as it relates to employee performance (Davenport & Prusak, 1998). Knowledge management systems are designed to identify and capture relevant information (knowledge) from expert employees, and then transfer that knowledge to those who need it in order to perform well, quite often the less experienced employees. One of the most useful functions of successful knowledge management systems is their ability to manage "just in time" learning requirements.

Just-in-time Knowledge Management

"Just in time" knowledge management systems specialize in providing just the needed information (knowledge) at just the right time to the requestor. For example, experienced maintenance personnel repairing complex machinery, such as an airplane, may need just a small amount of very specific information to complete their task, but they need it immediately. In a classroom, a student may be struggling to learn a new complex cognitive skill, such as using the second derivative to calculate the speed of a particle. A just-in-time system might recognize a point of difficulty that the student is experiencing and provide a helpful suggestion or a slight correction, enabling the student to learn the skill.

Just-in-time systems complement more traditional training

systems that provide knowledge "just in case" the student needs it at some point in the future. Typical classroom instruction falls into the just-in-case category, but a great deal of the knowledge may never be needed for actual practice, and students are typically less motivated for just-in-case instruction. This has led to the recognition of the value of just-in-time instruction, and instructional theory should take this into account.

Electronic Performance Support Systems

Electronic performance support systems (EPSSs) are a powerful tool for just-in-time learning. They can provide workers with just the right type of information (e.g. conceptual explanations, steps in a procedure, or past performance data) at just the right place (e.g. on the shop floor, as part of a computer software screen, or at the site of an experiment) in just the right amount and at just the right time. EPSSs can support levels of employee performance that may not normally be possible due to the complexity or sheer volume of information. This is an important function as many jobs increase in complexity and the volume of information increases in the Information Age.

EPSSs may be standalone systems or may be embedded in the performance tool itself. For example, an EPSS may be designed to assist teachers in choosing from among dozens of possible instructional theories and methods. Another form of EPSS is the "Help" system packaged as a menu selection in the main software package.

Embedded in Authentic Performance

Knowledge management systems are focused on authentic practice that is embedded in job performance. One of the main challenges in corporate training environments is to capture the corporate knowledge that is distributed (or shared) among the experienced employees and transfer that knowledge to newer, less experienced employees. The "communities of practice" perspective can facilitate this transfer of knowledge.

Communities of practice form when people carry out practices in social groups on a regular (and often frequent) basis. Communities of practice include members with varying levels of expertise, from the experts, who form the core of the community, to the novices, who are just starting to learn the practices of the community (Lave & Wenger, 1991). Sometimes, instructional designers are asked to "design" a community of practice. However, communities of practice are complex social organizations that are not well understood. Much more research and instructional theory development are needed.

Given the options for a knowledge management system to use communities of practice, EPSSs, or some other type of system, instructional theories are needed to help instructional designers decide which options to use and how to make best use of each.

Formative Research to Create Design Theory

Given the need to develop a wide variety of additional instructional theories for the Information Age, we would like to address the use of formative research to create such theories. The formative research methodology is a relatively new research method that can be used to create or improve existing design theory through testing its application in a specific case. This type of research aims to determine what methods work well in the theory, what methods don't work well and thus need to be improved, and how the design theory can be improved.

Formative research is a kind of case study research, action research, developmental research, and grounded theory development. The underlying logic of formative research, according to Reigeluth and Frick (1999), is that

> ... if you create an accurate application of an instructional-design theory (or model), then any weaknesses that are found in the application may reflect weaknesses in the theory, and any improvements identified for the application may reflect ways to improve the theory, at least for some subset of the situations for which the theory was intended. (p. 636)

In formative research, there are six major steps that the researcher follows (Reigeluth & Frick, 1999): 1) choose an existing design theory, or delimit the scope for a new theory; 2) design an instance (case) of the theory or select a case within the scope; 3) analyze the case in order to identify what works well and what needs to be improved; 4) identify improvements for the case based on formative evaluation data; 5) repeat the data collection for another part of the case or another case entirely, to explore whether the improvements generalize within the scope of the theory, and repeat the cycle again; and 6) suggest improvements for the design theory based on the experience of the case. There are variations in these steps depending on: a) whether the design theory already exists or is being developed from scratch, b) whether the case is created by the researcher or is/was created independently, and c) whether the case has already occurred or is occurring as the research is being conducted (Reigeluth & Frick, 1999).

Conclusion

As was indicated at the beginning of this chapter, instructional systems design is a field dedicated to helping people to do a better job of facilitating human learning and development of all kinds. This is a young field, and as we evolve deeper into the Information Age, instructional theories will be needed to offer guidance for taking full advantage of the opportunities that new technological developments afford to better meet the needs of individual learners.

REFERENCES

Ackoff, R. (1981). *Creating the corporate future*. New York: John Wiley & Sons.

ADL (2001). *Sharable content object reference model*. Available online: *http://www.adlnet.org/*. Last visited September 2002.

Anzalone, S., Sutaria, M., Desroches, R., and Visser, J. (1995). Multi-channel learning: A note on work in progress. *ED Journal*, 9(6), pp. J3-J7.

Ausubel, D.P. (1968). *Educational psychology: A cognitive view*. New York:

Holt, Rhinehart and Winston.

Banathy, B.H. (1991). *Systems design of education: A journey to create the future.* Englewood, NJ: Educational Technology Publications.

Barrows, H.S. (1986). A taxonomy of problem based learning methods. *Medical Education*, 20, 481-486.

Bates, T. (2001). *National strategies for e-learning in post-secondary education and training.* Paris: UNESCO International Institute for Educational Planning.

Beane, J.A. (1990). *Affect in the curriculum: Toward democracy, dignity, diversity.* New York: Teachers College, Columbia University.

Beatty, B.J. (2002). Social interaction in online learning: A situationalities framework for choosing instructional methods. Unpublished dissertation, Indiana University, June 2002.

Bell, D. (1973). *The coming of post-industrial society: A venture in social forecasting.* New York: Basic Books.

Bonk, C.J., & Cunningham, D.J. (1998). Searching for learner-centered, constructivist, and sociocultural components of collaborative educational learning tools. In C.J. Bonk & K.S. King (Eds.), *Electronic collaborators: Learner-centered technologies for literacy, apprenticeship, and discourse* (pp. 183-208). Mahwah, NJ: Lawrence Erlbaum Associates.

Cobb, P. (1994). Constructivism in mathematics and science education. *Educational Researcher*, 23(7), 4.

Corno, L. & Randi, J. (1999). A design theory for classroom instruction and self-regulated learning? In C.M. Reigeluth (Ed.), *Instructional-design theories and models: A new paradigm of instructional theory (Vol II)* (pp. 293-318). Mahwah, NJ: Lawrence Erlbaum Associates.

Cronbach, L.J., & Suppes, P. (Eds.) (1969). *Research for tomorrow's schools: Disciplined inquiry for education.* Toronto: Macmillan.

Davenport, T.H. & Prusak, L. (1998). *Working knowledge: How organizations manage what they know.* Boston: Harvard Business School Press.

Dick, W., & Carey, L. (1996). *The systematic design of instruction. 4th ed.* New York: Harper Collins.

Duffy, T.M., & Cunningham, D.J. (1996). Constructivism: Implications for the design and delivery of instruction. In D.H. Jonassen (Ed.), *Handbook of research for educational communications and technology: A project of the Association for Educational Communications and Technology* (pp. 438-456). New York: Simon & Shuster Macmillan.

Gagn'e R.M., & Briggs L.J. (1974). *Principles of instructional design.* New York: Holt, Rinehart & Winston.

Goleman, D. (1995). *Emotional intelligence: Why it can matter more than IQ.* New York: Bantam Books.

Gustafson, K.L., & Branch, R.M. (1997). *Survey of instructional development models. 3rd ed.* Syracuse, NY: ERIC Clearinghouse on Information and Technology.

Khan, B.H. (Ed.) (1997a). *Web-based instruction.* Englewood Cliffs, NJ: Educational Technology Publications, Inc.

Knowles, M.S. (1990). Fostering competence in self-directed learning. In R.M. Smith and Associates (Eds.), *Learning to learn across the lifespan* (pp 123-236). San Francisco: Jossey-Bass.

Koschmann, T. (Ed.) (1996). *CSCL: Theory and practice of an emerging paradigm.* Mahwah, NJ: Lawrence Erlbaum Associates.

Kuhn, T.S. (1996). *The structure of scientific revolutions, 3rd ed.* Chicago: University of Chicago Press.

Lave, J., & Wenger, E. (1991). *Situated learning: Legitimate peripheral participation.* Cambridge, UK: Cambridge University Press.

Lewis, C., Watson, M., & Schaps, E. (1999). Recapturing education's full mission: Educating for social, ethical, and intellectual development. In C.M. Reigeluth (Ed.), *Instructional-design theories and models: A new paradigm of instructional theory (Vol II).* (511-539). Mahwah, NJ: Lawrence Erlbaum Associates.

Martin, B.L., & Reigeluth, C.M. (1999). Affective education and the affective domain. In C.M. Reigeluth (Ed.), *Instructional-design theories and models: A new paradigm of instructional theory (Vol II)* (pp.485-509). Mahwah, NJ: Lawrence Erlbaum Associates.

Mayer, R.E. (1979). Can advance organizers influence meaningful learning? *Review of Educational Research.* 49, 371-383.

Merrill, M.D. (2000, in press). First principles of instruction. *Educational Technology Research and Development,*

Mukhopadhyay, M., & Parhar, M. (2001). Instructional design in multichannel learning systems. *British Journal of Educational Technology,* 32(5), 543-566.

Norman, D.A. (1976). *Memory and attention: An introduction to human information processing.* New York: John Wiley & Sons, Inc.

Pintrich, P.R. (1995). Understanding self-regulated learning. In P.R. Pintrich (Ed.), *Understanding self-regulated learning* (pp 3-12). San Francisco: Jossey-Bass

Reigeluth, C.M. (1983). Instructional design: What is it and why is it? In C.M. Reigeluth (Ed.), *Instructional-design theories and models: An overview of their current status* (pp.3-36). Hillsdale, NJ: Lawrence Erlbaum Associates.

Reigeluth, C.M. (Ed.) (1999). *Instructional-design theories and models: A new paradigm of instructional theory (Vol II).* Mahwah, NJ: Lawrence Erlbaum Associates.

Reigeluth, C.M., & Frick, T. (1999). Formative research: A methodology for creating and improving design theories. In C.M. Reigeluth (Ed.), *Instructional-design theories and models: A new paradigm of instructional theory (Vol II)* (pp.633-651). Mahwah, NJ: Lawrence Erlbaum Associates.

Reigeluth, C.M. (1994). The imperative for systemic change. In C. Reigeluth & R. Garfinkle (Eds.), *Systemic Change in Education*. Englewood Cliffs, NJ: Educational Technology Publications.

Reigeluth, C.M., & Merrill, M.D. (March, 1979). Classes of instructional variables. *Educational Technology*, 5-24.

Reigeluth, C.M., & Nelson, L.M. (1997). A new paradigm of ISD? In R.M. Branch & B.B Minor (Eds.), *Educational Media and Technology Yearbook*. Englewood, CO: Libraries Unlimited.

Savery, J., & Duffy, T. (1996). Problem-based learning: An instructional model and its constructivist framework. In B. Wilson (Ed.), *Constructivist learning environments: Case studies in instructional design* (pp. 135-148). Englewood Cliffs, NJ: Educational Technology Publications.

Siegel, M.A., & Kirkley, S.E. (1998). Adventure learning as a vision of the digital learning environment. In C.J. Bonk & K.S. King (Eds.), *Electronic collaborators: Learner-centered technologies for literacy, apprenticeship, and discourse* (pp. 341-364). Mahwah, NJ: Erlbaum.

Simon, H.A.(1969). *The sciences of the artificial*. Cambridge, MA: MIT Press.

Vygotsky, L.S. (1978). *Mind in society: The development of higher psychological processes*. Cambridge, MA: Harvard University.

Wiley, D. (2001). *The Instructional use of learning objects*. Bloomington, IN: The Agency for Instructional Technology and AECT.

3

Communication in Education

INGRID DAY

In 1999, the Commonwealth of Learning review of virtual education concluded that the impact and potential of educational technology was 'more rhetoric than reality'. In COL's follow up study, released two years later in July 2001, author Glen Farrell found that 'virtual education development is a lot more rhetorical' and also 'a lot more real".

That rapid shift in view previews well the difficulty in trying to pin down the state of virtual at present and (even more difficult) where it is headed. All one can hope to achieve is an informed picture of educational technology applications at present, and to speculate responsibly about where current trends are likely to head.

The COL authors (2001) assert that virtual education is now part of the planning agenda of most organizations concerned with education and training. In developed countries, this appears to be true - albeit with at times less pedagogical than bureaucratic clarity. As Farrell says

> *... this surging interest in virtual education ... remains largely focussed on ways to use technology to deliver the traditional educational products (i.e., programmes and courses) in ways that make them more accessible, flexible, and cheaper and that can generate revenues for the institution.*

Senior Lecturer in Communication Studies, University of South Australia, Australia.

The COL report makes an additional, important point that growth in virtual education is largely occurring in countries with mature economies and established information and communication infrastructure, and that developing countries have not yet used virtual education to bring mass education opportunities to their citizens.

In 1997, Turoff identified a number of key forces which are driving educational change. He suggested that students are becoming intelligent consumers, that the costs of tuition are rising, that public funds for higher education are decreasing, that the typical student is older, working, may have a family and will likely be a part time student, that geographical monopolies are disappearing and that administrators are seeking technology that will automate the delivery of material with a minimum of academic person power. He also argued that institutions with similar programs would be in very direct competition even though they may be thousands of miles apart.

In my experience these points are well-founded and in this discussion I am approaching Turoff's broad points from a 'grass roots' perspective. I should emphasise that this discussion simply expresses my personal views based on experience as an online educator. I have chosen this approach at least in part because I believe that too often the 'big picture' does not consider users with enough specificity. After six years teaching in the virtual as well as on-campus environment, there is one fundamental that I believe is too often overlooked: students still want people to be their teachers. They want personal interaction—not computer interaction. While this does not mitigate against online education—indeed it can be much more 'personal' than classroom teaching—it is often a factor that I believe is not recognised sufficiently by educational managers who may view the prospect of building technological infrastructures without a corresponding downsizing in staff as an unviable investment (although the use of information technology can mean significant savings in terms of physical spaces such as lecture theatres and libraries).

A further reason for considering both the users and providers of technologically-facilitated education is that technology is only as good as the use to which it is put—and the people who utilise it. These interrelated points are hardly new, but I believe that they are too often glossed over. If we do not truly recognise the centrality of people to virtual teaching and learning, then educational computing components will gather dust alongside the now sadly under-utilized videoconferencing facilities of the eighties.

First, we need to consider: 'What do students want from educational technology? I believe that for students, good teaching and learning fundamentals are the same as they have always been. To name just a few: teachers

- who communicate effectively,
- who set relevant assessment tasks to which they provide timely and thoughtful feedback,
- who generate interaction with peers,
- who design and align their classes and courses as much as is possible with applicable workplace outcomes, and
- who are passionate and care about student learning.

The Fundamental is People

What is not yet sufficiently recognized is that students are less and less excited by the simple idea of learning online. They have passed the 'forgive the technology and the teachers for their inadequacies because it is all so exciting' stage and they now pick and choose and evaluate online courses much more knowledgeably. We now have a population of sophisticated online learners rather than novices and trendsetters. And that is good! A discerning market raises standards—no longer is it acceptable to simply post lecture notes online or videoed lecture inserts on web pages.

Fewer and fewer people are enrolling in online courses whose only attraction is that they are available on the Web. And there are more and more takers for online education that is well planned, clearly presented, provides opportunities for various forms of interaction with teachers and classmates and that gives them substantive feedback on how they're progressing. Sound familiar? It is—student expectations of online learning are little different from their expectations of face to face learning. Technology alone is not enough.

Interestingly, just four years ago when my students were asked why they had enrolled in an online course, they would often respond 'to develop my web skills' and 'because it's new and different'. Very, very rarely are those comments made today. Now online courses are attracting students because the course has established a good reputation and because the teachers and the institution have a good reputation—and because they can access those three elements away from the campus. They need not be bound by geography and mobility to inferior educational opportunities. Turoff's (1997) prediction that students will seek information by which to evaluate their perspective purchases of courses and programs in my view has already been largely realised. That said—while students undoubtedly want flexibility in their access to learning (and qualifications), I do not believe that they want access at the cost of a 'real' person at the other end.

Another factor related to the increased opportunity for institutional and program selectivity which I believe will become increasingly evident over the next few years, is that course content is the least valuable asset of any learning institution. Economics 101 is essentially Economics 101 whether you are studying in Brussels or Brisbane—but the way that the course is taught and communicated and the reputation of the institution is critical. As delivery formats expand (and are combined and recombined in numerous ways) courses will be increasingly re-purposed for the ever more granularized student cohorts that it becomes possible to target (e.g. on a ship, in a plane, in the desert, fulltime workers, etc). Customising content for disparate learner groups is more and more achievable in terms of technological capacities—but the package needs to be delivered by people. We can clone the message but we cannot clone the messenger. As Turoff cautioned in 1997 'If a topic can be taught by software and there is no need for human communication... what we have [then is] training and the acquisition of skills'.

We need to remember that teachers are increasingly pressed to meet multiple demands including research, administration and teaching; and, as Bennett et al (1999) suggest, most academic staff have little or no personal experience either as online learners or teachers and as workloads increase and resources decrease, becoming conversant with a new technology may be a low priority. In my experience, teachers want transparent technology with a low learning curve; they want the same mobility as their students; they cannot cope with any significant increase in teaching time (often perceived as an outcome of LAAP (Learning Any Time Any Place) and they want support in spreading their teaching over various platforms. They want technology to facilitate rather than impede. Bates (1997) puts it well:

> *The most common form of training given to faculty is to show them how to use the technology. This though is starting at the wrong place. Many faculty need to understand why it is important to use technology for teaching in the first place. It has to be related to the changing environment in which universities find themselves, and in particular to the changing needs of learners.*

Bennet et al (1999) add that staff development should focus on enabling academics to connect the use of new technology to their own teaching experiences. In this respect the principles guiding academics toward the use of technology in their teaching catalogue is little different to good methodologies in teaching any student: make it relevant.

I believe that the next conventionally-utilised technology in education will be voice and video online environments for students and instructors. Classes will increasingly meet in real time to engage in synchronous voice discussion, deliver oral presentations to the class, the lecturer and invited guests; discuss assignment development using voice using file sharing capacities; engage in question and answer sessions; obtain immediate group feedback via survey; meet in breakout groups during class meetings and be able to record and edit a class to create an asynchronous session that can be accessed by students who missed class, and used in the future. While at present typical user (student) platforms are usually sophisticated enough to handle text and voice chat but are not yet viable for widespread video applications, as the technology advances video will be increasingly commonplace. At present there are great variations in the viability of software available to effect these synchronous, media-rich interactions with a simple interface, transparent technology and robust capacities. However, realistically priced platforms are increasingly becoming available and there will be a corresponding institutional uptake.

Voice and video-based applications will also extend teaching in the humanities in areas such as drama, dance, music etc. Courses where visual demonstration and evaluation is embedded in learning are increasingly viable in the web-based environment through the use of low cost webcams and microphones (at less than the price of some textbooks!). Interactive multimedia will become customary and the sense of innovation that is often evoked by the term now will fade. We will also be able to better serve varying student learning styles and the needs of students with disabilities as both text and audio will be available in online sessions and, as Coombs (1995) says students with disabilities can increasingly be mainstreamed via adapted computer technology. A further advantage (for all students), he adds, is that computer discussion tends to flatten relationships and decentralize power and reduce status barriers.

It is at times argued that synchronous learning platforms such as those I have described counter the notion of 'anytime any place' learning—which is often viewed as the cornerstone of virtual learning. When utilised as a replacement for on campus classes this is undoubtedly the case. When, however, used strategically to *enhance* 'any time' learning (rather than as a *substitute* for face to face classes) it will extend rather than inhibit the pedagogical possibilities. Too often, I believe, we model online educational environments on face-to-face teaching methods—minus the time and place scheduling. We also tend to oversimplify the potential impetuses and benefits of virtual education. Until we move on from conceptually constricted views and really begin to identify, implement and extend pedagogical possibilities in the online environment, the potential of technology will not be effect a legitimately 'new' educational paradigm. As Bates (1997) says:

> *...although there has been widespread adoption of new technologies for teaching in the last few years, they have yet to bring about major changes in the way teaching is organized and delivered. Without such changes, though, technology-based teaching will remain a marginalized activity, while at the same time leading to increased unit costs.*

These changes will come about in a gradual process of innovation, testing and uptake. Turoff predicted in 1997 that the distinction between distance students and regular students will disappear, in that local students will select when they wish to take a course via electronic technology or via the physical classroom. I believe this is already the case, just 5 years on. A decade from now 'convergence' will not be a term that has any significant currency in the educational lexicon.

To end on my original point. I believe that whichever crystal ball we gaze into we still see people reflected back at us. Once we recognise that people are at the heart of all communication (and teaching and learning is primarily about communication) educational methodologies and pedagogies and will move forward. Technology can only create an environment—success will lie with the people who use the environment with greater or lesser effectiveness in terms of teaching and learning outcomes.

REFERENCES

Andrewartha, Geoff and Wilmot, Simon (2001). 'Can multimedia meet tertiary educational needs better than the conventional lecture? A case study'. *Australian Journal of Educational Technology* 17(1), 1-20.

Bates, A.W. Restructuring the University for Technological Change. (*http://bates.cstudies.ubc.ca/carnegie/carnegie.html*)

Bennett, Sue; Priest, Ann-Marie and Macpherson, Colin (1999). 'Learning about online learning: An approach to staff development for university teachers' *Australian Journal of Educational Technology*, 15 (3), 207-221.

Chih-Hsiung Tu and Michael Corry 'Research in online learning community'. *Journal of Instructional Science and Technology.* Volume 5, number 1, April 2002. *http://www.usq.edu.au/electpub/e-jist/docs/html2002/chtu_frame.html*

Coombs, Norman (1995). 'What's so Hot about Distance Learning' *http://www.rit.edu/~nrcgsh*

Farrell, Glen (1999). *The Development of Virtual Education: A global perspective.* The Commonwealth of Learning. (*http://www.col.org/virtualed/index.htm*)

Farrell, Glen (2001). *The Changing Faces of Virtual Education.* The Commonwealth of Learning (*http://www.col.org/virtualed/*)

Laurillard, D. (1994) Multimedia and the changing experience of the learner, in M. Ryan (ed.) *Proceedings Asia Pacific Information Technology in Training and Education Conference and Exhibition*, APITITE 94. Brisbane, Aust. Vol 1: 19-24. *http://www.anu.edu.au/CEDAM/dl-apitite.html*

Lennon, J. & Maurer, H. (1994). Lecturing technology: A future with hypermedia. *Educational Technology*, April, 5-14.

Morgan, Chris and O'Reilly, Meg (1999). *Assessing Open and Distance Learners.* Kogan Page.

Nightingale et al (1996). 'Issues of teaching and Learning'. University of Western Australia. *http://www.csd.uwa.edu.au/newsletter/issue0398/grade.html*

Race, Phil (1995). 'The Art of Assessing'. *New Academic*, vol. 5 issue 3. *http://www.lgu.ac.uk/deliberations/assessment/artof_content.html*

Reeves, Tom (date unknown). 'Evaluating What Really Matters in Computer-Based Education'. *http://www.educationau.edu.au/archives/cp/reeves.htm*

The Massie Center. *http://www.masie.com/masie/default.cfm?page=default*

Turoff, Murray (1997). 'Alternative Futures for Distance Learning: The Force and the Darkside'. Keynote Presentation at UNESCO/OPEN UNIVERSITY International Colloquium, April 27-29: Virtual Learning Environments and the Role of the Teacher, Open University, Milton Keynes. (*http://eies.njit.edu/~turoff/Papers/darkaln.html*)

4

Multichannel Learning

STEVEN ANZALONE

The concept of multichannel learning grew out of a series of exchanges that took place throughout the world between 1993 and 1996 (Anzalone, 1995) following the World Conference on Education for All in Jomtien, Thailand in 1990. At the Conference, James Grant, then Executive Director of UNICEF, advanced the notion of the "third channel" as an underutilized avenue for developing education. Mr. Grant conceived of the third channel as the array of informal learning experiences coming through the use of traditional and modern means of communications. This was to be distinguished from the "first channel", consisting of formal schooling, and the "second channel" which includes organized, nonformal programmes. Despite the plea for greater reliance on this third channel, it proved difficult to translate the idea into programmatic terms (Mayo and Chieuw 1993). What proved to be more successful, however, was the idea of *multiple* channels as a means toward implementing the "expanded vision of basic education" enunciated at Jomtien (WCEFA 1990).

Later, the concept evolved through the activities of the International Multichannel Action Group for Education (IMAGE) launched by staff from UNICEF, the International Council for Distance Education, and the Education Development Center through the USAID LearnTech Project—and soon joined by UNESCO, the Commonwealth of Learning (COL), and other organizations. Main contention was to bring together partners interested in finding new ways to apply

---

Director, Educational Development Center, Washington D.C.

experiences from distance education, communications, and educational technology for advancing education for all. Moreover, multichannel learning grew out of the experience of interactive radio instruction and the evidence of its effectiveness to support basic education in developing countries (Bosch 1997, Dock and Helwig 1999, Leigh, Naidoo et al. 1995). Thus, we defined multichannel learning as *strategic orchestration of various means for mediated interaction that connect the learner with information, knowledge, and stimulation for the purpose of enabling learning.*

Multichannel Learning: Unpacking the Definition

Multichannel learning is about the relationship between education and learning. It places learning as the primary outcome of *organized* educational activities. These activities occur in both formal and nonformal settings. A multichannel approach recognizes the importance of informal learning that can be tapped in powerful ways to reinforce or extend organized learning activities or to make them more meaningful. Also, multichannel learning seeks to situate informal learning within a wider system—one that will guide growth in areas where learning is deemed to be so essential that it is pursued through organized social activity and not left to the effects of things such as individual maturation, intrinsic personal motivation, or chance.

The definition states that multichannel learning involves "strategic orchestration" of learning channels. Such orchestration grows out of proven and practical ways to go about designing and developing effective multichannel learning systems. This set of "know how" is open and flexible and not a fixed recipe of principles or procedures. Multichannel learning is an approach intended to be responsive to widely different conditions and possibilities found across the countries.

Implicit in the definition of multichannel learning is the important role played by the learning environment. Fundamental to multichannel learning is the idea that environments may be enriched in practical ways that are conducive to learning. The multichannel learning is about mediating connections between the learner and information, knowledge, and stimulation. Multichannel learning posits that an effective way to enrich learning environments is making them better connected, internally and externally. These connections—in the social rather than psychological sense—take place along paths or *channels*. Channels, which are discussed in more detail below, make use of persons, planned experiences, technologies, and materials that guide experience around information, knowledge, and stimulation.

What is distinctive about the multichannel learning approach is that it does not define quality in terms of whether x or y is being taught, whether x or y is being taught in a certain way, or whether the learning environment contains specific pieces of material input. Multichannel learning is not about the pieces of the educational programme but rather about the ways learners connect to them. In order to keep the multichannel learning approach in perspective, we look at these views before extending our discussion of multichannel learning concepts and procedures.

Substance and Flow in the Learning Environment

Snyder, Chapman, and Fuller (1992), in their study of classroom practice in Botswana, distinguished between *substance* and *flow*. *Substance* refers to *what* is to be taught. *Flow* refers to *how* it is taught and learned. The *how* includes ways the learning process is organized, managed, and guided.

Both substance and flow are important in an enriched learning environment. Substance reflects decisions about broad orientations of educational purpose and content, decisions about what subjects should be taught, and knowledge and beliefs about subject matter content. The last domain includes "more than just the facts, terms, and concepts of a discipline…(but also) the organizing ideas, connections among ideas, ways of thinking and arguing, and knowledge growth within the discipline.(Borko and Putnam 1996, p. 676.)

Most educational debates take place around substance issues. Debates on substance have focused on the perennial issue of the importance of basic skills versus higher order thinking skills or the priority to be assigned to "essential" subjects (e.g. math and science) versus subjects like art and physical education. Debate on substance often touches on contentious curriculum issues.

Flow in education is about *how* learning happens. There are far fewer public debates about flow than about substance. Some educational provisions like textbooks, libraries, and science labs, etc. lie in between substance and flow. Treated as surrogates for or repositories of substance, they are prescribed as inputs that should be "there." But viewed as flow, their value only emerges as something that is determined according to how it is used in relation to educational goals.

Multichannel learning follows from experience that demonstrates that although both substance and flow are important in the enriched learning environment, success is more likely to follow an approach of organizing around flow than around substance. This should not be taken as suggesting that substance does not need to improve or that it matters little.

Connections and the Learning Environment

The interplay of substance and flow takes place in the learning environment. Educational research demonstrates the importance of enriching the learning environment as a means for fostering the growth of understanding, competence, and identity in learners. A multichannel learning system seeks to enrich the learning environment through the architecture of channels that connect the learner to sources of information, knowledge, and stimulation.

The multichannel learning environment stresses the creation and strengthening of connections. This is important in three different ways. First, learning is the result of connections formed by the brain. As a result of stimulation, the brain forms connections between neurons. Because of learning, the number of connections increases and the pathways of neural connections become more richly complex. Second, learning results from the countless connections a person makes in daily life. Daily experiences, both organized and spontaneous, result in connections between information and knowledge from a multitude of sources. The proliferation of information and communications technology greatly expands the variety and location of these sources. Third, where learning results from taking part in organized, purposeful education, the chances that taking part in education leads to real learning are increased by the number and quality of connections that the learner is assisted in making by the environment in which he or she learns. A richer network of pathways and connections in the learning environment allows better flow—just as an efficient network of streets and highways allows better flow of traffic in a modern city.

Multichannel learning sees the task of creating or remodeling an effective learning environment as one of strengthening existing connections, activating new ones, and seeking combinations that reinforce and extend the learning experience. The multichannel learning environment is one where learners have more and varied paths to what is to be learned

Distinguishing between Connectors and Learning Channels

A learning channel is *a means for mediating interaction between a learner and information, knowledge, and other stimulation.* A learning channel is different from the channels found on television, radio or other communications technologies. Traditional channels have often functioned as highly capitalized pieces of real estate on the broadcast spectrum—assemblies of programmes provided in the light of varying degrees of commercial concern. Broadcast channels have functioned largely as one-way conduits for delivering programmes and messages. This reality is changing. Channels for communications are increasingly becoming characterized by two-way or multipoint communication—more like the telephone (with a conference call capability) than the traditional television. In the past, many people were linked to the wider world primarily through telephone, radio and television, one or two newspapers, the local movie theatre, and possibly some magazines. Most of the world's citizens still have access to information beyond their immediate environment through only a few communication channels. Anyone who has been even remotely conscious of world events knows that this situation is changing dramatically—even if unevenly throughout the world.

Both the traditional and newer communication channels provide a useful set of connectors for promoting learning. But there "no tech" connectors that also important. We will not attempt to catalogue the realm of potentially useful connectors that might be choreographed in support of learning, but we see the major categories as the following:

1. *People*—These include teachers, group leaders, mentors, fellow learners, and persons outside the immediate learning environment.
2. *Technologies*—Various configurations of broadcast, telecommunications, and computing technologies, including radio, television, telephone, computers, audio/video cassettes/CDs, and so on.
3. *Learning Materials*—These include "stand alone," discrete sources of information, including printed and electronic texts, pictures and moving images, graphical representations, and other aids to learning.
4. *Planned experiences*—These include community visits, field trips, school competitions, classroom projects, internships and other work experiences, debates, clubs, cultural activities, athletics, community service activities, and special events organized to promote learning.

Clearly, these categories sometimes overlap.

Learning channels, as we have mentioned, are more than just communications frequencies or other kinds of connectors. Learning channels are people, planned experiences, technologies, and materials *that mediate experience* around information, knowledge, and stimulation. What is distinctive about a learning channel is its function as a *mediator* rather than as merely a *source* of knowledge or information. A learning channel has two components: (a) an instrumental means for learners to make connections—again, we refer to these as connectors, and (b) a "programme" that makes use of these connectors in a way that actively mediates learning. Without the latter, the first remains simply a source or device—analogous to writing with a computer, something that most of us would be unable to do without a word processing programme.

Learning environments today are frequently characterized by this situation where the connectors function as "pipes and wires"—but carry little "water or electricity." For example, a library located near a school does not function as a learning channel for the school without a process to bring it "on line" in a way that guides learners to interact with the knowledge and information in a manner that leads to making meaning. In this example, the connector will not be effective if it functions simply to steer learners into proximity with the library's knowledge and information. Similarly, such things as textbooks left in the box or on the desk, text on the blackboard, and teachers' verbal representations remain as underutilized "inputs" and fall short of becoming true learning channels without the effort needed to make them serve as mediators of experience.

Channeling and Educational Purpose

The design of multichannel learning systems, as we have just argued requires transforming connectors into learning channels. This is only possible by proceeding from a clear sense of educational purpose and specificity as to the educational objectives that are to be achieved. Here, it is useful to remember the old adage that if we do not know where we want to go, almost any road will get us there. Below we offer some of the principal educational purposes that can be addressed through channeling strategies and that are commonly found in multichannel learning systems.

1. Channeling for Direct Instruction. Perhaps the most powerful educational purpose that can be achieved through effective use of learning channels is that of providing direct instruction for learners. This is efficacious for pre-primary, primary, and secondary school interventions as well as for programmes for older, out-of-school learners. In providing direct instruction, it is common for one channel to be used as a "lead channel," which provides the backbone for the learning experience. This channel could make use of radio or television programmes, print, or face-to-face to teaching. Usually supplementary channels are linked to the lead channel for purposes of reinforcement, providing complementary, alternative modes of learning, and to extend the scope of instruction beyond what can provided through the lead channel. The experience with interactive radio instruction demonstrates clearly how a direct instruction via radio learning channel produces significant results.
2. Channeling for Teacher Development and Direct Instruction. Interest is growing in multichannel designs to provide professional development experiences for teachers. One approach involves a direct instruction approach akin to what is described above. A second approach involves a strategy of combining a direct instruction to learners channel with a professional development learning channel. What is powerful about this combination is that professional development goes hand in hand with direct instruction. This allows for more direct and immediate understanding and application of new skills. This kind of channeling typically involves in a single programme two conversations, one with the learner, the other with the teacher. This must be carefully programmed in order to avoid confusion. The pioneering attempt to link teacher development with direct instruction through interactive radio came in

South Africa (Leigh, Naidoo et al. 1995). Perhaps the clearest example of combining two learning channels (one for the learner and the other for the professional caregiver) is the approach used in the interactive radio early childhood education programmes used in Bolivia, Nepal, and other countries (Bosch and Crespo 1995). Finally, experience in Guinea shows the utility of learning channels that guide professional development through exchanges among teachers as part of a school cluster approach.

3. Channeling for Community Education. Many interventions to support development of education now possess a component aimed at increasing parent participation or community involvement in the operation of local school systems. The rationale for this is largely to build community awareness of and support for education in order to foster increased willingness for communities to assume financial responsibility for operating schools. In countries where the capacity of central governments to increase their financial support for schools is lacking, such a strategy seems sensible, perhaps inevitable. Community participation as such fits easily as a component into the "inputs only" approaches to educational change described above.

A multichannel learning system provides the opportunity to get more value out of investments in community participation. This would result from widening the purpose of community participation to design activities in a way that community involvement functions as one or more learning channels. One channel might make use of nonformal adult education built around school and community development issues interlaced with entertainment. Such a community learning channel is planned for Haiti (Yasin and Lubérisse 1999). Another channel could make use of community members as a learning channel with the purpose or reinforcing and extending instruction for school children. Costa Rica has made use of this approach for environmental education (Vargas 1995). In both cases, careful programming is required to make them function effectively.

4. Channeling for Remediation. Multichannel learning systems offer possibilities to address the variation in learners' attainment. Channeling to achieve this purpose might do the following: (a) providing remedial channels to allow some learners the opportunity to catch up, (b) freeing up the teacher to work with smaller groups of learners by making available learning activities led through other channels, and (c) varying the nature of instruction to make it more accessible to learners that have difficulties learning through the means of a dominant channel (e.g. reading).
5. Channeling for Different Styles in Learning. In recent years, attention has been given to the idea of providing educational activities that accommodate a variety of learning *styles*. The notion of *styles* is used in a variety of ways—with varying degrees of research evidence for their justification. One is the idea of *cognitive style*. Cognitive style is defined as "an individual's preferred and habitual approach to organizing and representing information."(Riding and Rayner 1998, p. 8) According to this view, there are two principal dimensions to cognitive style, the holist-analytic style dimension and the verbal-imagery style dimension. The former dimension refers to individuals tending to organize information into wholes or parts. The latter dimension refers to individuals tending to represent information during thinking verbally or in mental pictures. The differences have significant implications for the way that material is structured and presented. Programming that takes into account differences between the learners with different cognitive styles will be helpful and something that can be realistically addressed (to varying degrees) in multichannel

learning systems.

6. Channeling and Formal/Nonformal Educational Distinctions. using a multichannel approach offers educators a framework where the boundary between formal and nonformal education is far less important. If educators begin to look more carefully at designing educational environments that promote greater flow and better connections for learners, this will inevitably lead toward using strategies, methods, and materials that transcend the designation as formal or nonformal. Effective multichannel learning systems will be those that remodel the learning environment in ways that provide more "non-instructional" learning channels through imaginative programming offered through media, planned experiences, and face-to-face connections.

We have just looked at six educational purposes that are typically addressed in multichannel learning systems. These purposes lie at the heart of effective educational design and in programming the use of learning channels. We now turn to the other important aspect of multichannel learning system design—the principles that assist effective learning.

Programmes with Principles

We have found several principles that are both strongly supported by research and by a wide consensus of opinion among educators everywhere.[1] We offer these below for the consideration of designers of multichannel learning systems.

1. Stimulating Active Learning. There is almost universal acceptance of the value of the active involvement of learners in educational activities. Divergent educational theories such as constructivism and

1. Some of these principles are derived from a list suggested by the Association for Supervision and Curriculum Development (ASCD 1999).

behavioural learning both assign importance to this but for different reasons. But few serious educators would make the case that active, meaningful learning is not something that should be pursued in favour of passive reception of knowledge transmitted by a teacher or other source.

2. Linking to Prior Knowledge. There is also broad consensus on the importance of linking new content to be learned to prior knowledge. This principle, however, is too frequently skipped over in designing learning activities. Effective multichannel learning practice routinely seeks to identify the "hook" to a learner's prior knowledge—either knowledge from something that has been previously taught or knowledge from daily experience.
3. Activating Comprehensible and Challenging Input. A third principle important for developing effective multichannel learning programmes is that of ensuring comprehensible input for learners. There are two aspects. First, such things as new concepts, vocabulary, and examples have to be carefully chosen in terms of where learners are known to operating—not where it is presumed that they are operating. Second, new input should be selected at a level just beyond what they currently know
4. Incorporating Variety. Providing variety across a multichannel learning system and in individual materials is another critical principle that needs to be underlined in good educational design. Stressing variety reflects an appreciation of the rapid mobility of learners' attention and the need for changing stimulus to attract attention.
5. Providing Useful Feedback. Good flow in the educational environment is multidirectional. An important part of the flow is the specific and timely feedback learners receive as they participate in learning activities. If feedback is too general, it

provides only "positive noise" and is of little value. If it is not timely, it cannot usefully guide the learner in building understanding or forming skilled behaviour. Developing the habit of incorporating feedback as one learns leads one to become a strategic learner. Multichannel learning systems seek to maximize the opportunities for specific, meaningful feedback from teachers/facilitators, media channels, print and other learning materials, and from other learners. The interactive radio instruction model offers examples and techniques how seemingly "one way" channels can be utilized to provide opportunities for feedback to learners.

6. Providing a Safe, Non-Threatening Environment. One important lesson from the research into what happens in the brain as we learn demonstrates the importance of safe, non-threatening environments in order to provide the necessary conditions for learning to take place. Experiencing insecurity or threatening conditions is likely to be associated with learners' undergoing the release of chemicals in the brain that blocks learning. There is now a clear biological basis for what has been traditionally a normative basis for good educational practice.

We believe that systematic application of the above-mentioned six principles of "good education" into the design and use of learning channels will almost certainly result in a learning system more effective than conventional activities. The list does not exhaust the variables that are important in the teaching/learning process or the principles that might be incorporated in locally-appropriate multichannel learning systems. In settings where there is room for more complexity in designs, one would also want to attend to principles such as high expectations for learners, increased time for engagement in learning, and improved educational leadership associated with the learning environment.

Multichannel Learning: A Framework for Practice

At the beginning, we mentioned that the multichannel learning approach consisted of both a conceptual and practical framework for developing effective strategies for teaching and learning. We have discussed the conceptual framework in the preceding pages and now look at the ways that multichannel learning may be put into practice. Again, we should note that the framework for putting multichannel learning into practice—something that has grown out of an eclectic mix of experience with interactive radio instruction, other educational technology, communication, and distance education—is not a recipe or a formal set of procedures. It will vary with the specific development intentions, educational and cultural conditions, and available resources.

Organizing to Do Multichannel Learning. Typically, multichannel learning systems and products are developed by multidisciplinary teams. The composition of teams reflects both the nature of what is to be taught and learned as well as practical considerations for involving relevant stakeholders in what is to be produced. Teams are made up of educational materials developers, curriculum or content specialists, media/"channel" specialists, research/evaluation specialists, teachers, and representatives of organizations that will collaborate in or sanction implementation. Some members of the team participate more actively at various points in the development process. But time after time, it has been shown that the prospects for developing and sustaining a successful programme are enhanced by ensuring that there is a broadly-based understanding of, and contribution to, the learning system that is to be developed. Such participation can be crucial, even when it means that participation and consensus building slows the development process.

Clarifying and Ratifying the Mandate. An essential, strategic aspect of developing a multichannel learning programme is to clarify and ratify the mandate for the programme. Where the programme calls for new content for a new audience, this may not be an issue. But where the programme becomes part of an existing curriculum, this *is* an issue. Many multichannel learning efforts have solved this by building agreements with key stakeholders that the new programme will not replace what may be an officially-sanctioned curriculum. Often, this means conceiving the programme as either an alternative or supplementary learning option—addressing the needs of an unserved part of the educational audience or providing the means to strengthen an existing curriculum. Whatever the case, the mandate must be clear. When links to an existing curriculum are required, mapping out those links is an important operational step. It is common that a multichannel learning activity follows an existing curriculum where objectives or content topics are stated in varying degrees of specificity. These provide the starting points for developing a multichannel learning package. The development process then proceeds to the specificity needed to develop effective lessons using the channels available. Depending on the situation, the work involves some manner of moving from content to skills to instructional strategies—with a focus on the needs and abilities of the audience and with a premium put on learning, not just on curriculum coverage.

Developing an Early Acquaintance with Intended Learners. Educators have much to learn from communicators in how they go about understanding their intended learners. It is still far too frequent that educators develop materials pitched to their perceptions of what students at a particular grade level should be able to do. Far too many print materials are developed for intended learners who lack the necessary background knowledge, comprehension skills, or vocabulary to understand and learn from the materials. Communicators are more likely to treat the characteristics of their audiences as something to be learned rather than as given. The development of multichannel learning programmes draws upon the strong tradition of audience research in the communications field. This is frequently done by an early testing of existing or prototype materials. Such testing helps determine the levels of difficulty for materials development (language, prior knowledge, and so forth) as well as points out areas where the use of other channels is necessary in order to introduce or reinforce content that is not easily understood.

Selecting a Combination of Channels. The multichannel learning development team needs to go through a process whereby the range of potential learning channels is envisioned and selected. This is a process of "extending" the range of possibilities—including those unutilized or underutilized. It also includes exploration of the prospects for adding new channels. Determining a feasible and manageable combination is done in light of existing conditions, resource availability, and the barometer reading of the local climate for change. In some places, traditional face to face instruction, print materials, and radio may be the only feasible combination. Others may find it feasible to incorporate other media or planned learning experiences. Still others may have the desire and resources to modify professional development channels. Whatever the combination selected, the learning development team needs to contain the necessary expertise to utilize designated channels. This may involve a division of labor across organizations and negotiating a framework for collaboration.

The process of selecting channels, together with the clarification of the curriculum "mandate" tends to suggest the overall scope of the multichannel learning system that can be developed. These can be specified in units, which contain specific numbers of media programmes, print materials, and so on. The determination of the number of learning units is largely dictated by resources and other practical considerations.

Determining and Applying Effective Learning Principles. As mentioned above, multichannel learning is consistent with a variety of principles that have been shown to be associated with effective learning. It is necessary that consensus be reached on a set of principles to be operationalized in the multichannel learning system and materials. We repeat our contention that experience shows that successful materials development is more likely to occur with a short, well-defined set of principles rather than with more ambitious and elaborate theoretical formulations.

The multichannel learning development process typically brings in subject area expertise following agreement on effective learning principles. Subject area specialists are asked to assist in generating a list of a breakdown of specific skills that are taught—and the usual methods for teaching them—in the subject at particular grade levels. Members of the development team look for ways to ensure that methods align with or are made to align with the effective learning principles. The subject area teaching consultation also seeks to look at how specific skills—methods constellations can be adapted, where necessary, for designated channels.

Developing Prototype Materials. Perhaps the best initiation into the development of a multichannel learning system is through the development of a few prototype materials. This provides real, hands on experience in operationalizing instructional objectives, translating objectives into activities, applying effective learning principles, making channels work together, and so on. Observing how and how well these materials work with the intended learners is usually quite illuminating for the development team.

Preparing a Master Plan. The foundation of an effective multichannel learning system is a well-defined master plan. The process of formulating a master plan brings together in a concrete fashion the steps just mentioned. The master plan becomes a blueprint to define the multichannel learning system and guide the entire development effort. The master plan consists of the learning objectives to be developed across the entire programme. Often, these are listed sequentially in the left hand column of a table. Across the top of a table are listed the learning units subdivided by the individual channels. Building the master plan fills in the cells of this table. Cells indicate where, when, and through what channel objectives are introduced, reinforced, and reviewed. The process of filling in cells invites planning on how channels will be made to work together.

The experience from the development of interactive radio instruction shows that establishing a well-articulated master plans is laborious—but the *sine qua non* for effective programme development.

Planning for Formative Evaluation. The strength of a multichannel learning system depends in large part on a continuous process of formative evaluation of learning materials. Formative evaluation is a function not of someone's judgment whether a material conforms to a preconceived notion of what learners should be able to do or how well the material conforms to an ideal curriculum. Rather, it is a function of how well it works with the learner. It is essential that a commitment is built to conducting regular formative evaluation and to either correcting materials (feedback) or compensating for shortcomings in subsequent materials (feed forward).

This brief discussion of suggested design steps give some idea of what it takes to initiate the process of developing a multichannel learning system. Needless to say, there are countless steps that cannot be discussed here that are required to complete the development and implementation of the system.

Conclusion

Multichannel learning offers a perspective that these challenges need not be dichotomized into "today" and "tomorrow" agendas for action. The concepts and practical procedures just discussed apply equally whether one is designing a system to reach learners in impoverished communities or a to connect learners to global information networks. But whatever the system to be designed, whatever the scale of resources that can be called upon by the learning environment, the need to make good use of channels for learning is the same. We believe that if educators can make effective use of those channels that are currently accessible, they will be well prepared to make effective use of those that become more accessible in the future. But it is important to keep in mind the difference between a technology and a learning channel. Technologies must be bent to serve educational purposes and not the other way round. To do otherwise risks hijacking educational development, turning learners into mere placeholders in the new dot-com culture and allowing potentially powerful tools for personal and social development to become empty boxes and fetishes of modernity.

REFERENCES

Anzalone, S., Ed. (1995). *Multichannel Learning: Connecting All to Education*. Washington, Education Development Center.

ASCD (1999). *Tape 1: Making Connections. The Brain and Reading*. Videotape. Alexandria, VA, Association for Supervision and Curriculum Development.

Bates, A.W.T. (1995). *Technology, Open Learning and Distance Education*. London, Routledge.

Borko, H. and R.T. Putnam (1996). Learning to Teach. *Handbook of Educational Psychology*. D.C. Berliner and R.C. Calfee. New York, Macmillan Library Reference USA.

Bosch, A. (1997). *Interactive Radio Instruction: Twenty-Three Years of Improving Educational Quality*. Washington, DC, The World Bank.

Bosch, A. and C. Crespo (1995). *Jugando en el Pidi: Active Learning, Early Childhood Development and Interactive Radio Instruction: Supporting Caregivers, Parents and Young Children*. Washington, DC, Education Development Center.

Dock, A. and J. Helwig, Eds. (1999). *Interactive Radio Instruction: Impact, Sustainability and Future Directions*. Washington, World Bank and U.S. Agency for International Development.

Heneveld, W. and H. Craig (1996). *Schools Count: World Bank Project Designs and the Quality of Primary Education in Sub-Saharan Africa*. Washington, DC, The World Bank.

Krashen, S.D. (1981). *Second Language Acquisition and Second Language Learning*. Oxford, Pergamon.

Leigh, S., G. Naidoo, et al. (1995). South Africa: Designing Multichannel Options for Educational Renewal. *Multichannel Learning: Connecting All to Education* S. Anzalone. Washington, DC, Education Development Center.

Mayo, J. and J.S. Chieuw (1993). *The Third Channel: Broadening Learning Horizons*. New York, UNICEF.

Moore, M.G. and G. Kearsley (1996). *Distance Education: A Systems View*. New York, Wadsworth Publishing Company.

Riding, R. and S. Rayner (1998). *Cognitive Styles and Learning Strategies*. London, David Fulton Publishers.

Snyder, C.W., Jr., D.W. Chapman, et al. (1992). Classroom Affect and Complexity: Ecological Perspective of Botswana Junior Secondary

Schools. *Advances in Educational Productivity*.D. W. Chapman and H.J. Walberg. Greenwich, Connecticut, JAI Press.

Vargas, G. (1995). *Multichannel Approaches in the Multigrade Classroom. Multichannel Learning: Connecting All to Education*.S. Anzalone. Washington, DC, Education Development Center.

World Conference on Education for All. (1990). *World Declaration on Education for All and Framework for Action to Meet Basic Learning Needs*. New York, Interagency Communication (UNDP, UNESCO, UNICEF, World Bank).

Yasin, K. and Y. Lubérisse (1999). *Meeting the Needs of a New Democracy: Multichannel Learning and Interactive Radio Instruction in Haiti*. Washington, DC, Advancing Basic Education and Literacy Project, United States Agency for International Development.

5

Interactive Videoconferencing for Instruction

DAVID A. TIEDEMANN

The technology currently used for videoconferencing has its roots in early television experiments conducted over 70 years ago. Over the intervening years technology and equipment has become generally more effective, reliable, portable, and affordable. As with many other technologies, business saw the advantages and implemented videoconferencing long before education did. Videoconferencing use in both business and education has been steadily increasing with much new interest being expressed after the September 11, 2001 World Trade Center tragedy. This is confirmed by the September 19, 2001 *Information Week Daily* electronic newsletter: "Analysts also believe the attacks' impact on transportation could drive interest in multimedia applications. 'I have heard some anecdotal stories from sources [vendors] who say they've seen a kick in usage,' says Andy Nilssen, a partner in Wainhouse Research" (George, 2001). There is no denying that videoconferencing is big business with nearly 4 billion dollars spent in the United States alone in 2000 (Greenemeier, 2001). Increasing robustness of Internet videoconferencing is spurring wider adoption in American education at all levels because it is less expensive and easier to use than early forms of videoconferencing.

Director, Faculty Computing and Media Services, Syracuse University, USA.

Definition and Technology of Interactive Video Conferencing

For this chapter, interactive videoconferencing is defined as synchronous two-way interactive video and audio communications, ideally conducted in a full duplex mode meaning that everyone in the conference can talk and be heard at the same time to better simulate normal conversation. "Ideally, a conferencing system provides the illusion that all of the participants are in the same room, sharing one space." (Duran and Sauer, 1997). According to Picciano (2001), "videoconferencing approximates the traditional classroom .... Instructors conduct classes, students can see the instructor, instructors can see the students, and students can ask questions of the instructor or each other" (p. 56). The emphasis is on building interactivity into their provision (Evans, Stacey, and Tregenza, 1999, p. 213) that takes educational television to the next level.

In the 1990s ISDN desktop (suitable for individual use) and conference room (suitable for small group use) videoconferencing systems was introduced by a few companies. These systems were designed to operate in compliance with the H.320 ISDN standard agreed upon in 1989 by the International Telecommunication Union - Telecommunications Standardization Sector (ITU-T), and the European Telecommunications Standards Institute (ETSI). Actually H.320 is a series of related standards for video compression/decompression, frame structure, data transmission, etc. Each ISDN line has two 64Kbps channels. Thus one, two, or three ISDN line videoconference calls use 128, 256, and 384Kbps bit rates, respectively. The ITU also established a family of H.323 standards for videoconferencing on local area networks and the Internet.

Both ISDN and IP videoconferencing systems use codecs (coder-decoders) to conserve the bandwidth used in a videoconference. Contemporary National Television Standards Committee (NTSC) analog television broadcasting in the North America, Japan, and other parts of the world uses approximately 90 Mbps bandwidth to transmit its 525 horizontal and 60 vertical lines of full motion video (e.g., 30 frames per second or fps), audio, and various control and test signals. Other regions of the world use Système Électronique pour Couleur avec Mémoire standards (SECAM) that transmits a 625-line vertical, 50-line horizontal display and Phase Alternating Line (PAL) with a 625-line vertical and 50-line horizontal display, both with slightly higher bandwidth requirements than NTSC.

"Internet-based videoconferencing has been in regular use since 1990" (Crowcraft, 1997, p. 159). One of the first widely available compressed video systems that allowed Internet video calls was the free software package, CUSeeMe created in 1993 by Cornell University (see: *http://www.cuseeme.com/*). Now, entry level IP videoconferencing can be had at no additional cost to those who already have a Windows computer and high speed Internet access. Microsoft provides free NetMeeting software that supports videoconferencing and application sharing (either bundled with Windows 2000 and XP operating systems or available for download from *http://www.microsoft.com/windows/NetMeeting/default.ASP* for use with Windows 95 and 98). Inexpensive video webcams (e.g., under US$50.00) can sometimes be purchased with a rebate that effectively reduces the cost to zero.

The high-water marks for Internet videoconferencing systems thus far have been the events know as the Mega-conference and Mega-conference II (Dixon, 2000). The first was held on October 11, 1999, with 60 universities and organizations from throughout the world participating. It was run from the Internet2 members meeting in Seattle, but since it was fully interactive, it occurred simultaneously throughout the world. Mega-conference II was run from the Internet2 members meeting in Atlanta, with 114 universities and organizations participating. Every continent except Africa was represented, including Antarctica (p. 26).

Internet access is opening up to even the most isolated locations through the use of satellite technology as used for the Megaconference II. For example, Very Small Aperture Terminal (VSAT) technology has been used by businesses since the late 1980s, primarily for credit card transactions. TEN (Trans-European Tele Education Network) is an example of a UNESCO backed VSAT effort in Europe. In TEN, a backbone VSAT network has been set up consisting of remote classrooms located one each in Portugal, Spain, Belgium, Ireland, the United Kingdom and Greece connected via satellite communications with the hub station. Lessons are given in English by a professor lecturing in the teacher's classroom located in the hub station in Madrid, Spain. TEN offers as a standard feature the possibility of combining videoconference and transmission of learning materials (slides, video, still images, text) in all courses (UNESCO, 1999).

Applications and Benefits

Interactive videoconferencing is but one of many instructional tools. Instructional videoconferencing can be seen from a perspective of cost effectiveness: "Just like economics, educational technology is continuously in search of greater cost-effectiveness—more and better learning for less and less amount of time and effort" (Mukhopadhyay, 1999, p. 130).

Given the versatility, the number of videoconferencing applications is limited only by one's imagination. Highlighted application samples include:

- Course delivery
- Supplement classes and training
- Guest lecturers or presentations
- Practitioner critique of student work
- Colleges can offer businesses employee training or certification programs
- Meetings
    - ❑ Interviews for student and faculty employment
    - ❑ Thesis and dissertation defense
    - ❑ Research brainstorming, problem solving, status reporting

- Collaboration for research, projects, publication, presentation planning, etc.

There are nearly as many educational videoconferencing benefits as there are applications. Examples of the most common benefits of interactive video conferencing follow:

- Overcome time and distance constraints
- Improve quality and spontaneity of guest lecturers or presenters
- Save time and money
- Overcome cultural barriers more easily
- Communicate directly with appropriate experts to enhance understanding of subject matter
- Multi-class courses or discussions to introduce different faculty, student, institutional, and regional expertise and perspectives
- Real-world contact can heighten student interest
- Students can take low enrollment courses that might not otherwise be offered
- Students can take classes not offered at their location
- Students can meet with tutors for enrichment and remediation
- Students isolated by distance or physical disabilities can take classes at a distance
- Teachers can team-teach with remote teachers sharing subject matter expertise or unique approaches to a topic

Perhaps the most common education application of interactive videoconferencing in many countries is the importing and exporting of guest lecturers greatly reducing the expense, inconvenience and, more importantly, downtime and lost productivity that is associated with the travel necessary to fly in a guest lecturer. The guest lecturer, being a credible real world expert or practitioner, adds relevance and quality to the topic being covered.

Given a trend of our multi-national world community conceptualizing itself more and more as a global village, one of the more important benefits of videoconferencing with its interactive visual and audio communication is its ability to help overcome cultural barriers. As with all forms of distance education, one of the greatest benefits of videoconferencing is the ability to reach students isolated by geography.

Barriers to Adopting Video Conferencing in Education

In a content analysis of 32 corporate distance education case studies, Cho and Berge (2002) identified 'the factors of organizational change and technical expertise, support and infrastructure' as the most frequent and influential barriers encountered" (p. 7). At the higher education level, Butler and Sellbom (2002) identify reliability of technology, time to learn to use new technologies, concern that technology's benefit may not be worth the effort, and lack of institutional support as the barriers (pp. 22-28). Some of the more significant barriers are ranked in an order that ranges from most difficult to easiest to surmount organizational, financial, time, and technological.

Organizational Barriers: Programs heavily dependent on videoconferencing can't succeed without a certain minimal level of organizational support in terms of vision, mission, priority setting, and leadership that encourages the formulation of effective policy to guide the program and procedures to implement it. Distance and the number or remote facilities and participating individuals multiply the difficulties. Education in general and higher education in particular is fraught with committees and task forces that often take months or even years to make significant decisions, some of which take longer to implement. Organizational cultures such as this support slow, measured change and avoid rapid, systemic change. The culture of the traditional classroom itself is a barrier to technology adoption. 'Difficulties in accessing hardware and software, the elaborate logistics involved in sharing a distant computer lab, lack of sufficient time during the school day, too little technical and instructional support for teachers—all these serve as deterrents to the use of technology….' (Hativa & Lesgold, p. 134-135). Once there is organizational support, progress in adopting technology then becomes, in part, a financial issue.

Financial Barriers: Cost is becoming less of a barrier to adoption of instructional videoconferencing with each passing year and the introduction of each new generation of videoconferencing hardware and software. In the mid-1990s a H.320 ISDN videoconferencing room system capable of a 512Kbps videoconference call cost around US$40,000. Five years later a more compact and capable H.320 and H.323 system could be obtained for about US$4,000—at one-tenth cost in less than five years. In 2002 "video appliances" such as Polycom's ViaVideo[2] can provide good quality 384Kbps, 30 video fps videoconferencing for around $500. There are, however indirect costs such as the monthly Internet access fee for an individual or the monthly access charges, network infrastructure, and technical support staff for an institution.

'The cyberstrikers in Brazil join Web surfers who have engaged in "Internet strikes" in Germany, France, Spain, the Czech Republic, China and Poland. Often organized by students and academics, the strikes are meant to protest high access charges, which can mount to hundreds of dollars in monthly Internet bills. The monthly cost of basic access in China runs $30 to $43, which is more than a quarter of the average monthly income according to the Guangzhou Daily, a newspaper' (Richtel, 1999, p. G3).

Then perhaps the question to ask is if it is cost-effective? "Interactive videoconferencing provides real time synchronous interaction between students and instructors and other students. It is a cost-effective means for incorporating speakers, electronic field trips, and subject matter experts into education" (Cavanaugh, 1998, p.15). Perraton (2000) takes the notion of educational technology cost effectiveness to a logical, but difficult and controversial conclusion of technology replacing teachers. A good cost effectiveness example is a large-scale

2. (see *http://www.polycom.com/products_services/products_groups/0,1422, 186-152-72,00.html*).

deployment of interactive one-way video, two-way audio satellite[3] distribution program for inservice education of primary teachers in India (Maheshwari and Raina, 1998). It may be added here that once the necessary infrastructures for interactive video technology are set up, the unit training cost using this mode will be favourable in comparison to that of the traditional face-to-face methodology (p. 98).

Time Barriers: The time required to adopt technology can be intimidating from both personal and institutional perspectives. If one is designing a new videoconferencing course, the effort to develop suitable techniques and supporting material may be considerable at first. However, the effort may be more daunting to transition existing materials appropriate for face-to-face instruction to ones that will work with videoconferencing's current limitations in, for example, resolution and aspect ratio. As Daunt (2001) suggests, faculty hesitate to spend the initial time required to effectively adopt new technology and thus do not enjoy the ultimate benefit of transitioning their materials.

Technological Barriers: Technical infrastructure, support, and expertise barriers revolve around adequate level of technical expertise, both for faculty and for support staff. If the video fails during a videoconference, one might get by with just the audio or a backup telephone call and speakerphone. If the audio fails in a videoconference, even with continuing video, one might as well cancel class and try again later. Clearly the failure of videoconferencing equipment whether for technical or operational reasons is intolerable for teachers, students, and support staff alike.

Just as technology can help overcome many of the barriers,

---

3. Editor's Note: Interactive One-way video-two-way audio conferencing is exensively used in India by several institutions, namely National Institute of Educational Planning and administration for capacity building of heads of educational institutions, Indira Gandhi National Open university for delivering a large number of distance education courses, All India Management Association for management courses, etc.

it introduces its own barriers. Lack of access to even basic videoconferencing resources is a technological barrier to more universal adoption of instructional videoconferencing, especially in developing countries. Insufficient resources, absence of reliable supply of electricity are the other barriers. Bandwidth can be another limiting technical factor in the adoption of videoconferencing. Although videoconferencing can be done with a 56Kbps modem, a broadband (cable modem or DSL connection) is generally considered the minimal bandwidth needed to support reasonable quality instructional videoconferencing.

Most of the limitations relate to difficulties in effectively replicating communication nuances that occur naturally in a face-to-face conversation in the videoconferencing environment. Some of these nuances are nonverbal e.g., subtle gestures that are lost in all but the highest resolution videoconferencing systems and conversational e.g., the side discussions that occur in a meeting (Buxton, Sellen. and Sheasby, 1997, p. 385).

Video Conferencing Effectiveness

Video Conferencing, with its full-duplex audio, live two-way video, and multimedia support, provides the closest match of all current distance-learning technologies to an in-person educational experience. From this perspective, videoconferencing is intuitively effective. Business, either through return on investment studies or an intuitive approach, has invested billions of dollars in developing videoconferencing capabilities for meetings, training, recruitment, certification, product announcements, etc. Probably few educational institutions have done formal return on investment studies before acquiring videoconferencing capabilities. Let us examine the issue in a few case histories, e.g. primary—secondary, higher education, collaboration between these levels, and cultural exchange, videoconferencing in developing nations, Syracuse University videoconferencing examples, and interactivity in videoconferencing.

Instructional effectiveness

After analyzing "...approximately four hundred scientifically designed and statistically treated comparisons of ITV and classroom teaching..." Wilbur Schramm (1962) states that the average student is likely to learn about as much from a television class as from ordinary classroom methods. In some cases he will learn more, and in some less, but over-all the conclusion has been 'no significant difference' (Schramm p 52,). Russell (1997) and Saba (2000) concurs with the plethora of 'no significant different' results. In the absence of such rigorous and relevant research results, one way to get a feel for the instructional effectiveness of videoconferencing is to review examples, successful and otherwise, in various settings.

Educational Videoconferencing Case Histories

Many schools, at all levels and in all regions of the world, have used videoconferencing, either satellite based from the 1970s to date or more recently compressed video systems over ISDN or IP connections. A few examples of educational videoconferencing applications documented in the literature are presented below.

Primary—Secondary Examples

"In Australia, Victoria has developed what is arguably the most widespread system-wide ITV provision of any similar school system in the world" (Evans, Stacey and Tregenza, 1999, p. 213). Much of the instruction in this Australian initiative is delivered via Science and Technology Education in Primary Schools (STEPS)[4]. Another Victoria initiative is Schools of the Future Network or SOFNet, as "...satellite-based, narrowcast ITV—was designated for use in primary (elementary) and secondary (high school) classroom settings, and how it collapsed as an endeavor (Evans, Stacey, and Tregenza, 2001, p. 1).

---

4. see: *http://www.sofweb.vic.edu.au/steps/*

Until 1998 students from anywhere in Victoria, and from a few ITV-connected schools in South Australia and New South Wales, were able to participate in each program live-to-air. They talked by phone with the teacher (presenter) in the studio. Somewhat contentiously, as is explained later, after 1998 the opportunities to interact were ceased or greatly curtailed to the extent that SOFNet became more of a video distribution network for schools to record their own video-cassettes of the programs (Evans, et al., 2001, pp. 3-4). The reasons given for the shift from interactive to more of a distribution role for SOFNet included: scheduling difficulties; program quality; late release of program notes, and discrepancies between the notes and than actual program which was distributed late. Organizational, rather than technological or other barriers seem to be responsible for SOFNet not achieving its full potential.

To overcome the isolation of very isolated (American) Cold Bay School and to improve its curricular opportunities, the school uses interactive videoconferencing to offer classes for which they have no teachers, such as Japanese or Spanish. These classes are imported from Spokane, Washington through STEP Star Network (see: *http://www.schoolaccess.net/*) via 256Kbps satellite access provided by GCI an integrated communication provider based in Anchorage. Students also use videoconferencing to interact with scientists participating with the Challenger Learning Center (*http://www.challenger.org/*). "In Cold bay, Alaska distance learning technology has increased academic rigor and broadened the curriculum" (Fratt, 2002, p. 26).

Higher Education Examples.

Two of many interesting higher education videoconferencing efforts presented here, are one each from the United Kingdom and Germany. In 1997 faculty from University of Paisley and Napier University in the United Kingdom studied a number of interactive videoconferencing applications. The applications included: "project management, dissemination, lecture courses, keynote lectures, small groups, orals and interviews" (Pitcher, Davidson, and Goldfinch, 2000). A six-hour calculus of variations lecture course delivered over three weeks by a Napier lecturer to six near end (on site) students and 13 students and a tutor at the far end Stirling University site (Pitcher et al., 2000, 201-202). They found videoconferencing to be effective, especially in small group settings.

A University of Koblenz-Landau Master of Arts Library Science major has a hybrid delivery option of Internet supplemented interactive videoconferencing through which students may enroll in courses taught at Humboldt University in Berlin. Regular videoconferences provide students at both the Koblenz and Landau locations (200 km apart) the opportunity to have personal contact with their Berlin based lecturers located more than 600 km away. Seminars, exercises, consultations and even examinations are conducted via videoconferencing (Kappel, et al., 2002, p. 9.)

Primary-Secondary/Higher Education Collaboration

There are important examples of collaboration between different levels of education. One such example is WADEN, the Wisconsin Association of Distance Education Networks, founded in 1997 (Jillson and Hannu, 2001, p. 213). WADEN's vision statement is, 'All residents of the State of Wisconsin will have equitable access to quality K-12, post secondary, and continuing adult education opportunities regardless of their physical location in the state, based upon the needs and expectations of the learner, instructor or citizen being served. Ultimately all distance education systems in the state will be interconnected electronically with the ability to acquire, at an affordable price, the appropriate technology needed for specific audio, video and data applications[5]

A more focused collaboration example is the Australia Virtual Workplace (see: *http://education.qut.edu.au/vwl/*) which partners a university teacher education program with six early childhood, primary and secondary schools via interactive videoconferencing of both pre-service teacher learning and in-

5. see: *http://www.uwex.edu/disted/waden/about/vision.htm*

school observations. Through the use of videoconferencing and web-based technologies, this two year (2001-2002) QUT project has created a 'Virtual Workplace' for both synchronous and asynchronous interaction between classroom teachers, preservice (student) teachers and staff of the Faculty of Education....Preservice teachers in the large lecture theatres at the Kelvin Grove Campus watch, via videoconference, live lessons being taught from school classrooms. They interact with the teachers before and after the lessons, participate in discussions in tutorials, and engage in question and answer sessions online on specific teaching and learning topics. In turn, the partner teachers and their schools benefit by extending their knowledge and use of the technical facilities for curriculum delivery and participating in professional development programs which are stimulated by a QUT Professional Development Facilitator (Cope, Lundin, and Albert, 2001, p. 1).

Cultural Exchange

As mentioned earlier, interactive videoconferencing can be an effective tool for exploring and learning about cultural differences. Three examples are presented, the first at the fourth-grade level. Two classes in Mexico City conducted school activities via videoconference with two classes in College Station, Texas in the United States. The need for collaboration was established through analysis of poems that students wrote about each other's cultures prior to any distance-learning activities" (Cifuentes and Murphy, 1999, p. 94). This example of cultural exchange was successful in terms of its positive cultural impact on students (Cifuentes and Murphy, 1999, p. 101).

A second example is at the high school level. Schools in England, Finland, Greece, Norway, Sweden, and the United States have joined together in a videoconferencing project so their secondary teachers and students can see and hear each other in real time and participate in cultural exchange. This monthly opportunity enables participants to exchange ideas, customs, feelings, and experiences related to the curriculum.

SAXophone (*S*tudents *A*ll over the world e*X*changing *o*ver the *phone*) began in 1995 as a volunteer project and has grown through word-of-mouth comments from participation by three schools to more than two dozen schools world-wide (Mizell, 1999, p. 102). SAXophone features holiday comparisons, electronic field trips, book readings and discussions with authors, etc.

Videoconferencing in Developing Nations

Distance education is much more utilized in many developing nations than it is in the United States. Several international agencies have been active in exploring, encouraging or promoting the use of open and distance learning in the developing countries. 'They include both general and specialised agencies: bodies like UNESCO and the European Commission on one hand and the Commonwealth of Learning and the Consortium International Francophone de Formation à Distance (CIFFAD) on the other, both of them set up to promote international cooperation through distance education (Perraton 2000) p. 153).

In India, UNESCO provided 70 television sets for community viewing and some portable generator sets for experimenting with television in some of the selected villages where there was no electricity. The first experimental television service was launched on 15 September 1959 to produce and transmit social education programmes under a project aided by UNESCO (Parhar 1999, p. 157).

A World Bank videoconferencing project is a "Global Integration and the New Trade Agenda for Africa" course, the goal of which is "To provide participants with an overview of the full range of trade and investment issues that are relevant to developing a successful strategy of integration into the regional and global economy" (World Bank Group, 2000). The course is designed to be delivered via ten weekly 2 ½ hour videoconferences supplemented by print and CD-ROM materials.

The Regional African Satellite Communications Organization (RASCOM) is an example of a major distance learning effort that is independent of international organizations and businesses.

Korea provides an Asian example of a focused national distance education effort. "In the 1990s, Korea developed and implemented the concept of 'Edutopia' intended to create an open and lifelong learning society" (Jung, March/April 2000, p. 48). Although much of the "Edutopia" effort is Internet and Web-based, there is a significant interactive videoconferencing effort. For example, the Korea National Open University (KNOU), created by the Seoul National University in 1972 (see *http://www.knou.ac.kr*), implemented a videoconferencing network in 1995 connecting 14 study centers; it introduced tutorial sessions, held meetings among university members in different places, encouraged open discussions among students, faculty members and general citizens, and created non-degree programs such as teacher training programs using the system (Jung, March/April 2000, p. 49).

Syracuse University Examples

Syracuse University (SU) uses videoconferencing for both research and teaching. A few examples are given below:

Research Examples

Two more recent research applications for videoconferencing at SU are summarized. The first was a series of ISDN videoconferences between SU physicists and their research collaborators in Brookhaven, NY and Paris, France. A cryogenic device used in the Paris laboratory had developed a leak that was impeding research progress and was difficult to troubleshoot. In three videoconferences, about two weeks apart, the physicists at all three sites simultaneously viewed blueprints on document cameras and shared ideas as to the cause of the leak in very interactive multi-language discussions. Between videoconferences, they would try out the solutions discussed, and then reconvene to discuss results and new ideas to try. By the third videoconference the leak was fixed and the research continued.

A current research use of videoconferencing at SU is also a teaching use. Senior engineering design classes at Cornell and Syracuse Universities work in a NASA funded Advanced Interactive Discovery Environment (AIDE). The fall 2001 courses meeting together were Design and Analysis of Aerospace Structures at Syracuse and Design Projects in Mechanical and Aerospace Engineering/Collaborative Distance Design of Structural Systems at Cornell. Although a topic of the classes is next generation space shuttle design, this use of IP videoconferencing is more about collaborative and multidisciplinary team based design. Dual screen data displays at both Syracuse and Cornell, and screen sharing software allow the live videoconference to be displayed simultaneously with drawings, PowerPoint, and other lecture/design support materials. One of the displays is a SmartBoard. The other screen generally shows the remote instructor, although there are times when it is used for student questions or student-student interactions. Lectures are recorded and made available on the Web for later use.

Teaching Examples

One of the earliest SU programs to make regular use of ISDN videoconferencing was the School of Management's Army Comptrollership Program[6]. About 25-30 active or reserve officers and civilians working in a comptroller capacity for or with the Army come to SU for each session. One of the primary methods of sharing the most up-to-date information with the students was to have experts from the Army, Department of Defense, General Accounting Office, etc. guest lecture on various topics. Prior to 1996, this meant flying in the guest lecturers or using telephone conference calls that lacked a needed visual element in this spreadsheet intensive curriculum.

6. see: *http://www.som.syr.edu/facstaff/army/suarmyrm/Acp.htm*

In 1996 the Army Comptrollership Program made frequent use of a centrally available videoconferencing system, and soon cost-justified acquiring one of its own. This program's use of videoconferencing has confirmed many of the benefits of videoconferencing discussed earlier, including: overcoming time and distance constraints; improving the quality and spontaneity of guest lecturers; saving time and money; and using real-world contact to improve student interest.

Some of the common threads in these videoconferencing case histories that made them effective are their characteristics of being interactive and curricular driven uses of the technology; involving real world practitioner critique; stressing active learning; and sharing a wider variety of viewpoints. From a cost-effectiveness perspective, videoconferenced guest lecturers have reduced travel and downtime expenses while facilitating more spontaneous and higher quality guest lecturers or presenters. From the course delivery perspective, exposure to different lecturers and students introduced multiple perspectives, often with regional differences, to enrich the dialogue.

The key to success is interactivity in videoconferencing. There are certain ground rules like maintaining personal connection with those at the far end using names, both personal and geographical and varying the pace of the presentation frequently. There are some personal qualities that promote interactivity in videoconferencing. An instructor who not only pays attention to the students but also shows interest is more engaging to far end students than a traditional lecture would be.

After a 1994 feasibility trial by Queensland University of Technology (QUT) teaching a masters level education course via videoconferencing, a project was implemented to study the degree of interactivity possible with this medium. Students from Hong Kong, New Guinea, and Australia participated in six weeks of face-to-face classes with two lecturers. Two of the students then returned to Hong Kong using three 90-minute videoconferencing sessions to complete the course. The project showed that a very high level of spontaneous interaction, comparable in effect to the on-campus situation, can be achieved and students at this level are able to maintain that interaction for long periods of time. This was contrary to current belief, espoused in the literature and training manuals, regarding videoconferencing which indicates that relatively strict processes, protocols and 'controls' are necessary for effective interaction (Burke, Lundin, and Daunt, 1997, p. 351).

Future

Mukhopadhyay (1999) comments on the future of educational technology in general and on Indian prospects for interactive video in particular, "The future of educational technology will depend essentially upon the future of the classrooms—their composition, ethos and even structure. There have been several discussions and debates on the emerging virtual classrooms, virtual schools, virtual campuses...The other technology which is steadily emerging and expanding at a much faster rate than expected is the satellite-based communication making interactive television with quality a reality" (pp. 138-139). There are both technology issues and societal concerns to be addressed in looking at the future of videoconferencing.

Technology Issues

VSAT satellite distribution systems are just beginning to evolve from their business beginnings in the 1980s to educational uses. We can look beyond VSAT technology to a new generation of Ka band satellites now being tested and expected to become commercially viable between in a 2002-04 timeframe. Combining VSAT, Ka-band, and the next generation satellite service with Internet2's speeds of in the vicinity of 9.6 Gbps (45,000 times faster than a 56K modem) will offer heretofore undreamed of videoconferencing capabilities in places not previously accessible.

One design possibility for future videoconferencing systems used by a small number of people is to for each participant to have their own display kiosk (PIP) displays. In simulating a four-way round-table meeting, the place that would otherwise be occupied by a remote participant is held by a camera, monitor and speaker....The net effect is that conversational acts such as gaze and head-turning are preserved because each participant occupies a distinct place on the desktop....Although there was no significant difference between the picture-in-picture PIP and Hydra approach with respect to some measures of turn-taking behaviour, Hydra did, as expected, support parallel and side conversations. NO such conversations were observed in the PIP approach (Buxton, et al., 1997, pp. 388-389).

Another videoconferencing system design intended to better simulate face-to-face discussion was called the Brady Bunch and was first tested in 1995. "The Brady Bunch was designed to be used in focused group interaction, where all group members play an active role in a discussion....the slow-scan images provide a sense of the context of the larger group and give group members who are not talking some presence in the meeting" (Buxton, et al. 1997, pp. 392-393). Some may recall the original Dick Tracy comic strip (a widely syndicated U.S. cartoon begun in the 1930s), 1935 radio show, or 1990 movie. Tracy began using a wristwatch sized videoconferencing device in the mid 1960s (Locher and Killian, 2002). With the recent introduction of videoconferencing capable cell phone/ PDA devices, a Dick Tracy type device may not be too far off in the future. There have already been several decades of experimentation with wearable computers and television cameras. It may be difficult to envision the sort of Star Trek holodeck-like videoconferencing, but it is not difficult to predict the availability of such technology in the not too distant future.

Societal Issues

While the digital and communications technology industries offer excellent products for a reasonable cost, distance learning providers, particularly those supported by public subsidies, need to be mindful that these products do not exist in many poorer people's homes. Nations that cooperate and invest billions of dollars in building a space station need to exert the same effort in resolving or at least alleviating the inequity that exists regarding access to what is increasingly being seen as important educational technology (Picciano 2001, p. 204). The first step of solving such digital divide is to acknowledge the problem. The first step to bridging the gap is to realize that technology has not benefited everyone equally, and begin to work on ways to level the playing field (Pearson, 2002, p. 19).

There are also privacy concerns as video cameras become smaller and wireless. For example, while having lunch with Steve Mann a colleague of the author was asked by him if it was all right for him to upload their image to the Internet. It would have been easy to do so without permission having been asked or given. However, others see the advances in videoconferencing as an opportunity to achieve a purer democracy: "Scaling conferences to millions, so that interactive Internet-based videoconferencing could replace bulletin boards, and perhaps be used for such large-scale phenomena as participatory democracy (rather than representative democracy), is another vision held by some Internet proponents" (Crowcraft, 1997, p. 538).

Regardless of how it is used in society at large, it is clear that videoconferencing technology will become more a part of every day life, in and out of academia. The potential is high for videoconferencing to become as integral to all aspects of life in the 21st century as the telephone did in the 20th century. Although his optimism for the impact of Picturephone was several decades premature, Dorros (1969) words seem more accurate in 2002, substituting the word videoconferencing for Picturephone: "A practical beginning has been made. Development of Picturephone service to its present stage brings the goal of better, more natural, and more nearly complete communication nearer to reality" (p. 141).

REFERENCES

Angiolillo, J.S., Blanchard H.E., Israelski, E.W., & Mané, A. (1997). Technology constraints of video-mediated communication. In K.E. Finn, A.J. Sellen, & S.B. Wilbur (Eds.), *Video-mediated communication* (pp. 51-73). Mahwah, NJ: Lawrence Erlbaum Associates.

Asian Development Bank. (2002, May). ADB harnesses ICT to fight poverty. (Manila, Philippines). (Retrieved: May 11, 2002: *http://www.adb.org/documents/news/2002/nr2002071.asp*)

Burke, C., Lundin, R., & Daunt, C. (1997). Pushing the boundaries of interaction in videoconferencing: A dialogical approach. *Distance Education*, 18(2), 350-361.

Butler, D.L. & Sellboom, M. (2002). Barriers to adopting technology for teaching and learning. *Educause Quarterly*, 25(2), 22-28.

Buxton, A.S., Sellen, A.J., & Sheasby, M.C. (1997). Interfaces for multiparty videoconferences. In K.E. Finn, A.J. Sellen, & S.B. Wilbur (Eds.), *Video-mediated communication* (pp. 51-73). Mahwah, NJ: Lawrence Erlbaum Associates.

Carpenter, C.R. & Greenhill, L.P. (1962). Facilities for instructional television". In the Institute for Communication Research, Stanford University (ed.), *Educational television: The next ten years* (pp. 286—332). Stanford, CA: The Institute for Communication Research, Stanford University.

Cavanaugh, C. (1998). The effectiveness of interactive distance education technologies in K-12 learning: A meta-analysis. (Doctoral dissertation, University of South Florida, 1998). *Dissertation Abstracts International*, 59, 2455.

Chen, A. (1998). *Internet-based videoconferencing in cross-cultural learning: A case study of an experiment between a Canadian school and a Chinese school*. Unpublished master's thesis, Queen's University, Kingston, Ontario, Canada.

Cho, S.K. & Berge, Z.L. (2002). Overcoming barriers to distance training and education. *Ed [Education at a Distance - the USDLA Journal]*, 16(1) (Retrieved on May 26, 2002: *http://www.usdla.org/html/journal/JAN02_Issue/article01.html*)

Cifuentes, L., & Murphy, K.L. (1999). Distance learning among Mexican and Texan children. *Educational Technology Research and Development*, 47(4), 94-102.

Conrad, R., Donaldson, A., & Knupfer, N.N. (2001). Activities to engage the online learner. *2001 Proceedings: Annual Conference on Distance Teaching and Learning*. (pp. 103-107) Madison, WI: University of Wisconsin.

Cope, R., Lundin, R., & Albert, L. (2001). Creating a virtual workplace for improving professional development on and off campus: A preliminary report from an ongoing odyssey. Queensland University of Technology, Australia. (Retrieved on June 1, 2002: *http://www.videolinq.qld.edu.au/Conference/2001/LT2001papers/CopeLundinVW.pdf*)

Crowcraft, J. (1997). Supporting videoconferencing on the Internet. In K.E. Finn, A.J. Sellen, & S.B. Wilbur (Eds.), *Video-mediated communication* (pp. 519-540). Mahwah, NJ: Lawrence Erlbaum Associates.

Daunt, C. (2001). enhancing videoconference teaching skills through innovative faculty development. *2001 Proceedings: Annual Conference on Distance Teaching and Learning*. (pp. 115-119). Madison, WI: University of Wisconsin.

Dixon, R.S. (2000). Internet videoconferencing: Coming to your campus soon! *Educause Quarterly*, 23(4), 22-27.

Dixon, R.S. (2002). Plans for megaconference IV. 5/14/02 email to Megaconference listserv.

Dorros, I. (1969). The evolution of PICTUREPHONE service. *Bell Laboratories Record*, 47, 137-141.

Duran, J. & Sauer, C. (1997). *mainstream videoconferencing: A developers guide to distance multimedia*. Reading, MA: Addison-Wesley Publishing Company.

Evans, T.D., Stacey, E., & Tregenza, K. (1999). An investigation of the development of dialogic approaches to teaching and learning in schools through interactive television. *Proceedings of ED-MEDIA World Conference on Educational Multimedia, Hypermedia & Telecommunications*. Charlottesville, VA: Association for the Advancement of Computing in Education, pp. 213-218.

Evans, T.D., Stacey, E., & Tregenza, K. (2001). Interactive television in schools: An Australian study of the tensions of educational technology and change. *International Review of Research in Open and Distance Learning*, 2(1), pp 1-16.

Fratt, L. (2002). Distance learning in a rural school. *Media & Methods*. 38(5) p. 26.

George, T. (2001, September 17) Travel concerns may prompt surge in videoconferencing. *Information Week*. (retrieved June 1, 2002: *http://www.informationweek.com/story/IWK20010917S0002*)

Gipe, T.S. (2001, January-February). Orbiting the dream: Satellites open new horizons for Africa's educators. *TechKnowLogia*, 2001, pp. 59-60. (retrieved on February 25, 2002: *www.TechKnowLogia.org*)

Greenemeier, L. (2001, April 23) Making videoconferencing cheaper, more reliable. *InformationWeek* (retrieved June 1, 2002: *http://www.informationweek.com/story/IWK20010423S0002*)

Hamamatsu Chamber of Commerce and Industry. (1998). Television: The pioneer of the picture period, Kenjiro Takayanagi. Hamamatsu, Japan: Hamamatsu Chamber of Commerce and Industry. (Retrieved 6/14/02: *http://www.hamamatsu-cci.or.jp/industry/number_one/03_tv/03e_tv.html*)

Hativa, N. & Lesgold, A. (1996). Situational effects in classroom technology: Unfulfilled expectations and unexpected outcomes. In S.T. Kerr (ed.) *Technology and the future of schooling. Ninety-fifth yearbook of the National Society for the Study of Education, part II.* (pp.131-171). Chicago, IL: University of Chicago Press.

Hull, R.B. (1962). A note on the history behind ETV. In the Institute for Communication Research, Stanford University (ed.), *Educational television: The next ten years* (pp. 334-345). Stanford, CA: The Institute for Communication Research, Stanford University.

Jillson, C. & Hannu, R. (2001). Interactive television in the Badger State: A partnership for learners! *2001 Proceedings: Annual Conference on Distance Teaching and Learning*. (pp. 213-215). Madison, WI: University of Wisconsin.

Jung, I. (2000, March-April). Korea: Can edutopia become a reality?" *TechKnowLogia*, pp. 48-50. (retrieved on February 25, 2002: *www.TechKnowLogia.org*)

Kappel, H., Lehman, B., & Loeper, J. (2002). Distance education at conventional universities in Germany. *International Review of Research in Open and Distance Learning*, 2(2). (retrieved April 4, 2002: *http://www.irrodl.org/content/v2.2/loeper.html*)

Lanier, J. (2001, April). Virtually there: Three-dimensional tele-immersion may eventually bring thc world to your desk. *Scientific American*. (Retrieved June 2, 2002: *http://www.sciam.com/2001/0401issue/0401lanier.html*)

Locher, D., & Killian, M. (2002). Dick Tracy: About the comic. Chicago, IL: Tribune Media Services, (Retrieved June 6, 2002: *http://www.comicspage.com/dicktracy/aboutcomic.html*)

McVicker, D. (2001, January 17). Satellites go IP. *Internetweek.com*. (retrieved May 26, 2002: *http://www.internetweek.com/indepth01/indepth011701.htm*)

McVicker, D. (2001, January 22). Satellites defined. *Internetweek.com*. (retrieved June 2, 2002: *http://www.internetweek.com/indepth01/indepth012201.htm*)

Maheshwari, A.N. & Raina, V.K. (1998), Inservice training of primary teachers through interactive video technology: An Indian experience. *International Review of Education*. 44(1), pp. 87-101)

Mainzer, E.A. (1984). *AT&T Picturephone: The dysfunctionality of a functional structure*. New York: New York University.

Mizell, A.P. (1999). Creating a small, small world through videoconferencing: SAXophone. *Educational Technology Research and Development*. 47(4), pp. 102-107.

Mukhopadhyay, M. (1999). Educational technology. in M. Mukhopadhyay & M. Parhar (eds.) *Indian education: Developments since independence*. (pp. 130-141). New Delhi: Vikas Publishing House.

Noor, A.K. (2001). Pathway to our future engineering workforce. (Syracuse, NY: Syracuse University). (retrieved June 8, 2002: *http://www.i2sports.com/events/2001q4/nasa/*)

Orwell, G. (1983). *1984: A novel*. New York: New American Library,

Parhar, M. (1999). Media in education: Developments in India. in M. Mukhopadhyay & M. Parhar (eds.) *Indian education: Developments since independence*. (pp. 154-163). New Delhi: Vikas Publishing House.

Pearson, T. (2002, March / April). Falling behind: A technology crisis facing minority students. *TechTrends*, 46 (2), pp, 15-20.

Perraton, H. (2000). *Open and distance learning in the developing world*. London: Routledge.

Peters, J. (1985). *A History of television*. Geneva, Switzerland: European Broadcasting Union. (Retrieved 6 / 14 / 02: *http://www.dvb.org/resources/pdf/history-tv.pdf*)

Picciano, A.G. (2001). *Distance learning: Making connections across virtual space and time*. Upper Saddle River, NJ: Merrill Prentice Hall.

Pitcher, N., Davidson, K., & Goldfinch, J. (2000). Videoconferencing in higher education. *Innovations in Education and Training International*, 37 (3), pp.199-209.

Richtel, M. (1999, January 14). Overseas Internet users protest high cost of access. *The New York Times*, p. G3.

Rosen, E. (1996). *Personal videoconferencing*. Greenwich, CT: Manning Publications Co.

Russell, T.L. (1999). *The no significant difference phenomenon*. Raleigh, NC: North Carolina State University. (also see: *http://teleeducation.nb.ca/nosignificantdifference/*)

Ryan-Nicholls, K. (2001). Why choose interactive instructional television? *Quarterly Review of Distance Education*. 2(4), pp. 367-375.

Saba, F. (2000). Research in distance education: A status report. *International Review of Research in Open and Distance Learning*, 1(1), pp. 1-9.

Schram, W. (1962). What we know about learning from instructional television. In the Institute for Communication Research, Stanford University (ed.), *Educational television: The next ten years* (pp. 52-76). Stanford, CA: The Institute for Communication Research, Stanford University.

UNESCO. (1999). Trans-European tele education network. pp. 1-5. (New York: UNESCO). (retrieved May 26, 2002: *http://www.unesco.org/webworld/build_info/ten.html*)

Video Development Initiative. (2000). *Video conferencing cookbook*. Version 2.0 (Atlanta, GA: Georgia Institute of Technology). (retrieved May 26, 2002: *http://www.vide.gatech.edu/cookbook2.0/*)

World Bank Group. (2001, August 2). Australia, World Bank unveil virtual

Colombo plan. (Washington, DC: The World Bank). (retrieved February 25, 2002: *http://wbln0018.worldbank.org/news/pressrelease.nsf/673fa6c5a2d50a67852565e200692a79/ecc0ac73e7b4768785256a9c0052c57 0? OpenDocument*)

World Bank Group. (2000, November 29). Global integration and the new trade agenda for Africa course outline. (Washington, DC: The World Bank). (retrieved June 11, 2002: *http://www1.worldbank.org/wbiep/trade/DL_Africa.html*)

Yermish, I. (2000). A case for case studies via video-conferencing. In L.K. Lau (ed.) *Distance learning technologies: Issues, trends and opportunities.* (pp. 208-217). Hershey, PA: Idea Group Publishing.

Young, J. (2002, May 3). Self-described 'cyborg" reveals promise and dangers of wearable computers. *Chronicle of Higher Education*, 48(34), A31.

6

Online Education

ALISON A. CARR-CHELLMAN

There are a variety of compelling issues which frame the current debate around online education in the university. Issues such as quality of instruction, fiscal implications, open access, and intellectual property remain entirely unresolved in most communities. These issues and several others are of vital importance for careful consideration by faculty, students, administrators and the general public who funds higher education through tax dollars. This chapter presents several of the most compelling and hotly debated issues in online higher education today. By framing each topic in the language of their advocates as well as their skeptics, I hope to create a powerful argument which will help move this debate to a higher level.

Online Education on the Rise

For many faculty today, distance education may seem of relatively little concern. Because online learning still remains a limited endeavour at most universities, faculty, for the most part, have not taken an active interest in the issues associated with online learning and its potential impact on the university. However, online learning is rapidly becoming ubiquitous in higher education (Mendels, 2000; Arenson, 1998). The most recent Department of Education survey shows an increase of 72 per cent in the number of distance education programs (Carnevale, 2000). More than one third of all four-year colleges and universities offered some form of distance education in 1997 (National Center for Education Statistics, 1997) and the

Professor-In-Charge, Instructional Systems Penn State University, USA offerings are on the rise. In general, public institutions are joining faster than private institutions and larger institutions faster than smaller ones. Traditional distance education entities such as the University of Phoenix are enjoying a huge rise in enrollments (more than 22% in 1999) and these enrollments are concentrated in online distance education programs (Carlson, 1999). In addition, a variety of forms of university-corporate partnerships are becoming increasingly common (e.g., Blumenstyk, 1999b, Beckman, 1999).

As of May, 1998, more than a hundred degrees were available on-line from humanities to aerospace engineering (World Wide Web Learning Community, 1998). Many of these degrees are available from traditional institutions such as the University of Maryland, Ohio University, Auburn University and California State University. The growth in web-based education is an explosion unparalleled elsewhere in the educational enterprise (Daniel, 1996; Jones, 1997). Fueled by fear of open-market competition and recent advances in web-based design tools, the economies of scale for distance education have become very attractive to higher education administration. While web-based degree offerings proliferate, the impacts on the broader system of higher education are not at all clear. I now turn to a more detailed exploration of several issues in an effort to show the complex nature of the online learning enterprise. It is hoped that this discussion will promote a healthy skepticism among faculty for what is currently a largely unquestioned movement (Hara & Kling, 1999).

Quality and Content

Advocates

One of the most natural questions that is raised regarding online education (or any educational innovation) is whether it is *as* effective or *more* effective than what is currently in place. In the case of online education, several comparison studies have been conducted and more are being undertaken to show that online learning produces equivalent or superior educational results to traditional face-to-face instruction. A typical example of such research is Hiltz's examination of the use of asynchronous learning networks (ALN) in college level courses (1997). Hiltz finds that, "Overall ratings of courses by students who complete ALN based courses are equal or superior to those for traditional courses. Dropout or Incomplete outcomes are somewhat more prevalent, while grade distributions for those who complete tend to be similar to those for traditional courses."

In a recent study of school administrators engaged in an online program at the University of Montana, Foster (1997) found that *everyone* in the program had expanded their understanding of professional and personal qualities needed by effective school administrators. Gubernik & Ebeling (1997) report on a study conducted by the University of Phoenix in which standardized achievement tests were given to graduates of bachelors degree programs from their university and from three competing Arizona public institutions. They found, on average, the on-line students scored 5-10 per cent higher than their traditional residential counterparts.

While these studies may be seen as either compelling or self-serving, the quality issue is not prominent in the current debate. Instead, most advocates build their arguments more on the needs of the students for convenient, practical, skills-oriented learning opportunities. Some advocates rely on efficiency or access as their justifications, but few right now are trying to suggest that in fact the actual educational worth is higher than face-to-face. Some advocates are suggesting that for certain students, the online format allows for increased interaction from students who typically remain quiet in the traditional classroom (Perelman, 1994).

Skeptics

It is not clear that the findings of comparison studies are valid and reliable. Research on distance education in general, and web-based distance learning in particular, has not been conducted in systematically useful ways. In her critique of distance education studies, Blumenstyk (1999) calls prior distance education studies "questionable". Russell (1999) completed a comprehensive examination of more than 400 media comparison studies in distance learning and found that in general, there is not a significant difference between these media suggesting that there may not be any concrete educational *advantages* in web-based learning. While Russell is an advocate of distance education, and admits he was seeking confirmation that distance education was a better form of delivery, he was unable to find supporting empirical evidence of that assertion.

Very few skeptical studies have emerged in the area of online learning. Perhaps the most well-known is the Hara & Kling (1999) study of a small online graduate course which resulted in a high incidence of student frustration. Currently there is not overwhelming or compelling evidence on either side to suggest that distance learning is an effective substitution for face-to-face instruction. This is not to suggest that we should not continue to conduct a variety of qualitative and quantitative studies to further understand the effectiveness of online learning, but rather that the generally positive, pro-innovation nature of most current research in online learning is worthy of critical analysis.

While many distance education studies conducted to date focus on the *differences* between the media and, sometimes, their effects on learning, theorists in instructional technology (e.g., Clark 1994) have suggested that we shift our focus away from studies which simply compare the effectiveness of various media and toward a deeper understanding of the characteristics of any given media. The argument here is that certain types of learning lend themselves to certain characteristics of any given media and instructional technologists are searching for pedagogically appropriate matches. This leads us to the question of content areas being proliferated in online learning. The Internet's characteristics lend themselves to information dispensation and the efficiency goals of most online learning programs require large online "classrooms" (much like lectures which also support information dispensation). However, in many instances we are trying to make the online media carry instruction which does not match its fundamental characteristics of effective information dispensation. Recent reports of teaching law (Mangan, 1999), counseling (Sampson, Kolodinsky, & Greeno, 1997), history (Jaschik, 2000), and even physical fitness and exercise (Carr, 1999) online call into question the pedagogical rationale used in determining which content areas will be carried over the wires.

Efficiency

Advocates

Efficiency and democratic access are perhaps the primary justifications for web-based education offered by advocates. Advocates argue that public financing for higher education is being dramatically cut at the same time that the children of baby-boomers are arriving at the university threshold (Jones, 1997). In addition, the paying customers of higher education are increasingly budget minded (Daniel, 1996). As early as 1997 advocates (Hettinger, 1997) were pointing to cost savings as one of the important reasons to create the online learning enterprise,

> A Western Governor's University goal is cost savings for students as well as educators through increased competition...WGU enjoys the advantage of low overhead. 'We don't have a faculty. We don't' have a campus.' Students probably won't see lower course fees but will save on such associated costs as transportation and child care. Utah Governor Mike Leavitt told a congressional committee last spring that an online university can provide lower-cost education than a conventional university, though he did not provide specifics. (Hettinger, 1997, 21)

One of the common themes that runs through this part of the debate is the pressure on higher education to respond to workplace needs and budget crunches. Silvio (1998) describes this temptation.

> Some of its (online education's) possibilities are the reduction of operating costs for teaching and learning programs, increased control of learning by the learner, more interactivity...individually paced learning and lifelong learning...All of this seems very tempting to higher education, which is so very pressured by the exceedingly high demands made upon it by society." (8).

Some of the advocates recognize that the efficiency argument outweighs even quality arguments (Gubernik & Ebeling, 1997). Jones (1997), who is the founder of Jones University, one of the first virtual institutions to gain state level accreditation writes,

While there will never be a substitute for the ivy-covered experience of the college campus, advances in computers, cable television and satellites and the ubiquitousness of the Internet and its World Wide Web should and will make higher education available to the most people at the lowest cost—worldwide. (45).

In order to best meet efficiency goals, it is necessary for online education to limit itself to primarily information dispensation for economies of scale and simplicity. There are those, however, who feel that efficiency is an issue that is out of alignment with the educational goals of institutions of higher education.

Skeptics

Perhaps one of the most compelling skeptics for the efficiency argument is Michael Berube (1998). In his recent editorial, "Why inefficiency is good for universities" published in the *Chronicle of Higher Education*, he suggests that the efficiency equation requires a consequent loss of quality of experience,

> When you're 'teaching' 10,000 students by satellite or over the Internet, there's no way you can read and grade their papers, counsel them on their courses, work with

> them on their prospective careers, or write them letters of recommendation for jobs and postgraduate programs. Personal, individual contact with students is one of the most costly and inefficient services a university can provide. It is also one of the most valuable—and the most educational....

Indeed, on-line degree programs have the potential to be efficient; however, the impact on effectiveness and quality is not effectively addressed by advocates of web-based education. Despite its significant market demand and its apparent utility, web-based education is not without its critics (Drucker, 1995; Galusha, 1998; Noble, 1998). The idea that an on-line educational experience may be qualitatively different and one-dimensional despite similar or better test scores, for instance, is not typically a part of the equation for determining their value. The impact on the university as a place; the university environment and culture as a whole (Drucker, 1995) does not currently enter into the efficiency calculation.

Some theorists are already asking the question, is distance education really an efficient means of facilitating learning? The Internet has shown that it can be a good way to disseminate information, but the information may not be reliable and almost everyone who has spent time surfing the web knows the inefficient use of time spent to find information among the huge storehouses of data currently available online. David Noble (1998) has pointed out that the economics of online education really do not pan out as well as administrators had hoped. In order to make online education work efficiently, large numbers of students must enroll in courses and degree programs taught by relatively few faculty assisted by teachers aides. While our public institutions warehouse freshmen and sophomores in large lecture halls, parents and the public decry the lack of education possible in such an approach. Many institutions are, therefore, encouraging faculty to teach smaller undergraduate courses. Now some distance educators and administrators wish to extend that large lecture model into graduate education as the Masters Degrees in many vocational areas are the hottest selling online education ticket today.

Most faculty involved in these degree programs recognize that learners need a high level of interaction and attempt to build that into their courses, requiring certain numbers of postings to listserve discussions and such. However, this approach is time consuming for students and faculty who may get hundreds of postings daily, many of which are redundant or compliant without substantively discussing a topic. To replicate the many interactions that typically take place in a graduate classroom, the connection that a faculty member carefully fosters among her students, the in-depth feedback offered for student assignments—all this is difficult if not impossible online.

Advocates suggest that we should not be replicating current modes of learning online, but should discover what types of learning the medium best facilitates and design instructional environments which capitalize on web-based advantages while minimizing its disadvantages. The medium is an efficient and relatively effective dispenser of information, but as yet, it has not proven to be an efficient learning facilitator. Richard Sclove articulates what many of us familiar with the Internet already suspect,

> I find the Web useful when I have a conceptual framework built up already, and I just need a few little factoids to plug in to illustrate points. The Web is marvelous for that. But it's not a vehicle for building up depth of intellectual understanding. The extent to which students rely on the Web as their primary learning vehicle is deeply troubling. (Sclove, 1998, 15)

Instead of asking what the Internet allows us to effectively do (dispense information) and designing instruction to fit that medium because it is efficient or glitzy or fundable, we should instead be asking how do people best learn a given topic, and create learning environments on- and off-line that meet those learning needs.

The assertion that online education is efficient is related to the assertion that online education is also more democratic. If the purpose of expenditures to build online learning infrastructures is democracy, then costs should not be an issue. The advancement of a democratic learning system which truly reaches out to all, and advocates for all, regardless of ability to pay should prevail. However, in a somewhat contradictory stance, cost effectiveness and democracy are both used by advocates as primary justifications for the initial technology investment.

In such a marketplace of vocational education opportunities, what will happen to those courses on Shakespeare, Kant, and Impressionist painters? What will happen to unpopular, unmarketable, and non-vocationally oriented ideas? Higher education has always been the bastion of unpopular ideas. As a public institution, higher education may have fallen away from making itself relevant to the public, but it has always maintained a space for even the most politically incorrect ideas. Can this ideal survive in the face of online education, tightening budgets and corporate capitalism's continued encroachment on our university culture?

As Winner (1998) points out, "State legislatures would now rather invest in digital bandwidth than spend money on conventional settings for teaching and learning." (9) If we consider how best to invest public monies currently being spent on technology and marketing for online education, it might seem anti-change or even Luddite-esque to suggest that we revert to more support for conventional learning environments. On the other hand, it may not be too much of a stretch to suggest that where there are twice as many marketers and managers as teachers and instructional designers (as is too often the case in many Continuing and Distance Education Departments), we may have a misalignment in terms of the mission of an educational institution. Since the monies must come from somewhere, and the most likely proposition is a redistribution of funds already available for traditional initiatives, the fiscal implications of online programs are substantial and disconcerting. If we cannot be assured that the promises of democracy and efficiency will be delivered, in the face of concerns over shifting the burden for expensive corporate training from private to public funds, why should we shift monies away from traditional instructional functions?

In the end, as Berube points out so eloquently, learning is usually a very labor intensive process—a highly inefficient process. Putting education online does not change that fact unless we plan to make qualitative shifts in the nature of higher education to take the labor out of it. Thus it has not been shown conclusively that online education is inherently more efficient, and therefore we should continue to study and question this assertion.

Who owns it?

Perhaps the most hotly contested terrain in the online learning discussion today is the area of intellectual property (Young, 1999; Carnevale, & Young, 1999). The university was relatively unprepared for the online revolution and did not have appropriate policies to govern the ownership of online courseware. Noble (1998) reports on the issue of copyright, ownership, and faculty reactions to these issues in the online world in his original "Digital Diploma Mills." In it, he writes,

> Once faculty put their course material online, moreover, the knowledge and course design skill embodied in that material is taken out of their possession, transferred to the machinery and placed in the hands of the administration. The administration is now in a position to hire less skilled, and hence cheaper, workers to deliver the technologically prepackaged course. It also allows the administration, which claims ownership of this commodity, to peddle the course elsewhere without the original designer's involvement or even knowledge, much less financial interest. (9)

Most universities, and particularly divisions of continuing education would like to maintain total control and ownership over courses developed for online delivery. But faculty who have been stung by the video course fiasco of the 1980's in which courses were delivered repeatedly, in essence eliminating the need for faculty, are leery of such agreements and many are refusing to sign away all rights. In some cases, the universities assert "work for hire" contract stipulations to capture ownership rights, while faculty assert intellectual property rights of their own. Using old models of patents, funded research, or consulting seem to be outmoded and not able to keep up with the current maelstrom surrounding the issue of who owns, and therefore who controls the future distribution and use of courses developed for online delivery.

There are no simple solutions to this problem, naturally the AAUP wants more faculty input into distance education program design and implementation while university administrators want to maintain as much control over the courses as possible and individual faculty typically want only to ensure that what goes out onto the wires with their name on it is relatively updated and appropriately utilized. There are no research studies which can guide us in this debate, there are only a few positions which seem highly self-serving at the current moment. Ultimately the resolution will come over time through many negotiations between various faculty, unions, and administrators across the nation at many different types of institutions of higher education. While it may seem that distance education is still a relatively small scope enterprise, the foundations of the rules we will live by are being laid. As faculty, we should concern ourselves with these policies and actively engage in the negotiations to ensure that all members of the university community, particularly students, are protected and honoured and that no member of the community is taken advantage of.

Time and System Implications

Social isolation among Internet users is being increasingly pointed to as a source of depression and declining social interaction (Taha & Callwell, 1993; Sleek, 1998; Kraut, etl.al, 1998). So, in the name of lifelong learning, or keeping a job, workers are being asked to forgo leisure time with their families and friends and, instead, update their skills through the web. This pressure is part of the reformulation of capitalist culture in what is largely understood as the postmodern era. Simpson (1995) points out, "Postmodernism's emphasis upon novelty colludes with capitalism's interest in proliferating and expanding desire and with the technological promise of satisfaction. The 'good life' that technology tends to deliver is one of 'endless novelty, change, and excitement,... unlimited possibility,' in short, just the speedup of life that is characteristic of postmodernism." (153)

Simpson's main emphasis is on the ways we use technology to overcome time. This is clearly the case in distance education, "technology's ability to shrink space and time is often viewed only instrumentally, that is, as being merely the ability to decrease by degrees the 'distance' separating the desiring subject and the object of desire, and to do so without in any significant way altering the subject or the object." (Simpson, 1995, 3) However, we are not at all clear that this collapsing of time and space do not alter the learner, the faculty, the content, or the university in critical ways.

In my experience teaching distance courses, most distance education students come to the activity because they want pragmatic answers that they can apply to their full time jobs. Distance programs do not seem to attract students who are interested in immersing themselves in a field of study or learning about theoretical constructs, history of the field, background information and the like. Perhaps because of the marketing which emphasizes convenience and real-world learning, or because of these well-intentioned students' conflicting goals to work full time and go to school while also raising a family, the distance learner is not well suited to traditional residential degree program objectives, particularly at the doctoral level. To the extent that traditional brand-name universities offer online degree programs in addition to their residential programs, they are likely to have a dramatic impact on faculty and student lives.

The system-wide implications of such a shift are substantial. Recent studies of Internet experiences indicate increased isolation, (Sleek, 1998) access equity gaps, (Gladieux & Swail, 1999) and questionable quality (Thurber & Pope, 1998) of distance education programs. To the extent that we are merely placing raw information—lecture notes—on the web, we are often replicating the worst of traditional university learning experiences at a distance. The concerns and skepticism over the potential commoditization of higher education appear well justified. Distance education unfettered has the potential to relegate universities to a role in our society devoid of all the hallmarks of a community of scholars. Unpopular ideas may die out completely as a result of a lack of marketability in the wide and fast moving online education movement. University programs may become increasingly vocational in nature, focusing on an ever changing array of "hot topics" Differentiated staffing is likely with a few highly paid faculty performers, making information dispensation entertaining while masses of poorly paid part time instructors, graders, tutors and the like maintain direct contact with students.

We may try to move away from this model in residential instruction, making face-to-face higher education more labour intensive with smaller undergraduate classes. Meanwhile we are relegating many adult learners who are lured by the promise of career advancement to a labour-poor, information-rich learning experience. The actual effect of this is to free up more monies to make high quality residential education even more exclusive for those who can afford to attend, while working and middle class learners are served by a distance learning system and the poorest have no access at all.

Naturally, none of these predictions may come to pass depending on the extent to which distance education is implemented and diffused throughout the system and how well distance degrees are accepted by faculty, students, employers and graduate schools. However, the underlying cause of the rapid proliferation of distance education will not have disappeared. The fact is, the university is making itself into a business and operating in more business-like ways every day. And faculty everywhere are accepting the increased involvement of corporations in curriculum and research directions. While faculty bemoan the lack of funding available in higher education, millions are spent on new technologies and infrastructure. This is money that might be spent making the case to the public that the university is still a relevant and important public institution that needs maintenance if it is to survive. And amidst the institutional conflict between business goals and educational missions, the university administration puzzles at the lack of loyalty among faculty that their institutions inspire. I believe that we must pay attention to the underlying corporate model of an efficient industrial-age university and fight against university policies made based on profit motives.

At the very least, faculty would be well-advised to strongly advocate for some differentiation between traditional residential instruction and distance education. The history of correspondence courses (Noble, 2000) should have taught us that firewalls between the university and distance learning are a necessary, if elitist, evil which is likely to advance not detract from the goals of democracy in higher education. If we allow no differentiation, then administrators and legislators feel that education equals information dispensation and there are no differences between residential and online education. If we, as faculty members, suspect that there *are* indeed differences, then we must defend the right of all, the poor, the diverse, the under-served, to equal access to quality, funded educational opportunities. Distance education cannot become the bone we throw to those who cannot qualify for increasingly scarce scholarship dollars. While distance education administrators may see an undifferentiated transcript in which all courses have the same names and numbers regardless of modality as progressive, it can aggravate alumni (Daniel, 1996) and create confusion in the marketplace for students.

Conclusion

The future of distance education needs to be carefully shaped. Faculty and distance education administrators need to be savvy about distance education offerings. If we choose to continue down this path, there are several specific concerns that we should consider as we move ahead:

- Corporatization of the curriculum
- Equal access to technology among haves and have nots
- Pressures on learners and potentials for isolation and depression
- Elimination of unpopular or unmarketable ideas
- Efficiency of labor-rich distance learning programs
- Learning effectiveness of information-rich distance learning experiences
- Reallocation of budgets toward technology and away from traditional residential instruction
- Appropriateness of student population for goals of graduate degrees
- Expectations of learners based on advertisements for distance learning
- Differentiated staffing patterns
- Vocational curriculum emphases
- Economies of small college towns
- Promulgation of the poorest forms of instruction
- Aggravation and confusion among graduates of residential programs
- Effects on diversity of learning groups and learners' confrontation with that diversity
- Copyright and intellectual property issues

Certainly, this list is not exhaustive and we'll learn much as a result of our first steps into online learning.

For faculty in today's university setting, many pressures are constantly being balanced. The pressures to publish or perish, to increase class enrollments, to deliver excellent educational experiences, to advise students well about their futures, to make money for the university through grants or conducting distance education courses, and not least of all, the pressure to make an important contribution to the body of knowledge in an academic field. None of these pressures are likely to dissipate in the coming years. Some of them will become increasingly difficult to resist. Given the recent tendency of institutions of higher education to continually move toward business models of operation, the pressures to increase efficiency, productivity, and profit generation will likely become more heavily emphasized. Because of this, faculty must become clear about their roles, personally and collectively, in the institution of higher education. They must be smart, not just intelligent, about the way they conduct their business particularly where distance education is concerned.

REFERENCES

Beer, M. Feeding Hungry Minds. *San Francisco Examiner*, May 16, (1999): 2.

Berube, M. (1998). Why inefficiency is good for universities. *Chronicle of Higher Education*, March 27, 1998.

Carnevale, D. & Young, J.R. (1999). Who owns on-line courses? Colleges and professors start to sort it out. *Chronicle of Higher Education* December, 17, 1999; A5.

Chomsky, N. Propaganda and Control of the Public Mind. In R.W. McChesney, et. al. (eds.), *Capitalism and the Information Age: The Political Economy of the Global Communication Revolution*, New York: Monthly Review Press, 1998.

Daniel, J.S. *Mega-universities and Knowledge Media: Technology Strategies for Higher Education*. London: Kogan Page, 1996.

Drucker, S.J. Distance Learning and Education as Place. *Telematics and Informatics*, 12 (2), 1995: 69-73.

Foster, L A Collaborative Distance Graduate Degree Program: A Case Study for Building the Professional Community within Schools. Paper presented at Annual Meeting of American Association of Colleges of Teacher Education (49th, Phoenix, AZ, February 26-March 1),1997.

Galusha, J.M. *Barriers to Distance Education*. 1998. ERIC Document # ED 416 377.

Gladieux, L.E. & Swail, W.S. *The Virtual University and Educational Opportunity*. Washington, DC: The College Board. 1999.

Gubernick, L., and Ebeling, A. I Got My Degree Through E-mail. *Forbes*, 12, June 16, 1997: 15.

Hall, J.W. The Revolution in Electronic Technology and the Modern University: The Convergence of Means. *Educom Review*, 30(4), 1995: 1-7.

Hettinger, J. Degree by E-mail. *Techniques*, October, 1997: 21-23.

Hiltz, S.R. and Wellman, B. Asynchronous Learning Networks as a Virtual Classroom. *Communications of the ACM*, 40, (9), 1997: 44-49.

Jones, G.R. *Cyberschools*. Englewood, CO: Jones Digital Century, Inc. 1997.

Kraut, P., Patterson, M., Lundmark, V., Kiesler, S., Mukhopadhyay, T, Scherlis, W., Internet Paradox: A Social Technology that Reduces Social Involvement and Psychological Well-being? *American Psychologist*, 53(9), 1998:1017-1031.

Kirschkop, K. Democracy and the New Technologies. In R.W. McChesney, et. al. (eds.), *Capitalism and the Information Age: The Political Economy of the Global Communication Revolution*, New York: Monthly Review Press, 1998.

McChesney, R.W., Wood, E.M., and Foster, J.B. (Eds.). *Capitalism and the Information Age: The Political Economy of the Global Communication Revolution*. New York: Monthly Review Press, 1998.

National Center for Education Statistics' Report, *Distance Education in Higher Education Institutions*. October, 1997.

Noble, D.F. Digital Diploma Mills part IV: Rehearsal for the Revolution. 2000. Available online: http://www.XX

Noble, D.F. Selling Academe to the Technology Industry. *Thought and Action*, Spring, 1998: 29-40.

Noble, D.F. Digital Diploma Mills: The Automation of Higher Education. 1997. Available online: http://www.XX

Olsen, F. 'Virtual' Institutions Challenge Accreditors to Devise New Ways of Measuring Quality. *The Chronicle of Higher Education*, August 6, 1999: A30.

Perelman, L. (1994). As quoted in Echoes of a conference: Excerpts from EDUCOM '93. *Educom Review*, 29 (1), 1997. 1-7.

Postman, N. *The End of Education: Redefining the Value of Schooling*. New York: Knopf, 1995.

Sclove, R. The Democratic Uses of Technology. *Thought and Action*, Spring, 1998: 9-18.

Silvio, J. The Virtualization of Universities: Improving the Quality of Academic Work. INET '98 Conference Proceedings. Available online: *http://www.isoc.org/inet98/proceedings/4f/4f* 2htm. April 11, 1999. The Internet Summit, Geneva, Switzerland, 1998.

Simpson, L.C., *Technology Time and the Conversations of Modernity*. New York: Routledge, 1995.

Sleek, S. Isolation Increases with Internet Use. *American Psychological Monitor*, 29 (9), 1998: 1, 30-31.

Taha, L.H, and Callwell, B.S. Social Isolation and Integration in Electronic Environments. *Behaviour and Information Technology*, 12(5) 1993: 276-283.

Thurber, B.D., and Pope, J.W., Electronic Communication and the Humanities. INET '98 Conference Proceedings. Available online: *http://www.isoc.org/inet98/proceedings/4f/4f* 2htm. April 11, 1999. The Internet Summit, Geneva, Switzerland, 1998.

World Wide Learning Community Website [On-line], Available: *http://www.wwlc.com/*. 1998.

Winner, L. Tech Knowledge Review *Netfuture: Technology and Human Responsibility*, 72, June 2, 1998: 4-10.

Young, J. (1999). A debate over ownership of on-line courses erupts at Drexel. *Chronicle of Higher Education*, April 2, 1999.

7

Educational Technologies, Open Learning and Optimizing Learning

COLIN LATCHEM* and ALLAN HERRMANN**

Had India's universities of the early 20th century heeded the urgings of Nobel laureate Rabindranath Tagore to open up their courses to home-based students living outside their geographical boundaries, the sub-continent would have joined the UK, USA and Australia in pioneering open learning. Unfortunately, institutional recalcitrance prevented Tagore's vision from being realized within his lifetime (Mukherjee, 1997) although it is now manifest in the work of Indira Gandhi National Open University (IGNOU), the state open universities and the correspondence course institutes. Tagore's vision is an issue we shall return to at the end of this chapter.

From Correspondence Education to Open Learning

Open learning is commonly held to have its origins in the 'correspondence education' introduced into England in 1840 by Sir Isaac Pitman when he saw the commercial opportunities in training the burgeoning numbers of office workers in his new Stenographic Soundhand system (Rumble, 1997). Those enrolling in these courses received training packages, transcribed passages into shorthand according to the printed instructions, submitted their work for assessment, received feedback, and then proceeded with the next exercise. Subsequent forms of distance and open education have followed this basic methodology, although not always in such an inflexible 'lockstep' or 'one size fits all' manner.

---

*Former Head Teaching Learning Group, Curtin University of Technology, Western Australia, Australia , **Faculty of Education, Deakin University, Australia

The idea of opening up educational opportunities for self-sufficient and resourceful autodidacts may also be traced back to the Chinese imperial examination system, which operated from the Sui Dynasty (589-618 AD) until the early 20th century (Ren, 1998). This embodied the Confucian principle of openness to class mobility and was designed to circumvent the possibility of nepotism and corruption in selecting candidates for the mandarin class. The final examinations were highly competitive but open to all and so promising candidates unable to attend formal institutions were encouraged to study on their own, developing the necessary calligraphic and literary skills and mastery of the works of Confucius and his disciples (Cheng, Jin & Gu, 1998). Accreditation was granted to those who could demonstrate that they could successfully apply these teachings to the current affairs of state. The mode of learning, time taken in completing the course, or number of examination re-sits were not important (Cheng, 1998)—nor indeed was age: the oldest recorded graduate was 98 (Liu, 1996).

By contrast, Pitman's and the other correspondence schools were purely for-profit institutions. Many of these offered courses and services of dubious quality, making their profits from the up-front payments, high dropout rates, and low piecemeal rates paid to their casual teaching staff. The early years of the 20th century saw voluntary regulation of correspondence education in the US and Europe and there has subsequently been enormous improvement in the quality of open and distance education, some of which enjoys parity of esteem with more traditional forms of education, nationally and internationally. However, thanks to the poor reputation of the earlier correspondence education, there is still a lingering perception within some countries, official bodies and members of the public that open and distance education is 'second rate', 'second best' (Rumble & Latchem, in press) or even a 'rip off' (Boshier & Pratt, 1997).

Today, an ever growing number of conventional face-to-face institutions are incorporating the methods and technologies of open learning into their curricula to accommodate the needs of new generations of learners, and the open universities and colleges are showing just how many 'second chance' learners are capable of mastering new learning and improving their qualifications and job prospects.

Open learning (known as distributed learning in North America) uses a combination of presentational methods and constructivism and enables learners and teachers to interact synchronously or asynchronously across classrooms, workplaces and other settings, increasingly, but not exclusively, by means of information and communications technology (ICT) (Dede, 2000). Open learning is best looked upon as an approach to learning rather than a particular system or technique. It is based upon the needs of the individual learner rather than the interests of the teacher or institution. It gives the students as much control as possible over_the what and when and where and how of their learning. It uses the delivery methods of distance education and the facilities of educational technology, and it changes the role of the teacher from a source of knowledge to a manager or facilitator of learning (Johnson, 1994). Students who opt for this mode of learning, which can be provided wholly or partly off-campus, typically do so for reasons of work, family, disability or economic circumstance or because they are so far away from the providing institution.

Open learning takes different forms in different contexts. It is shaped by circumstances (socio-economic, political, technological, etc.) and intent (learners to be served, methods and materials to be used, content to be mastered, etc.). It may involve any, or any combination of, the following:

- alternative admission requirements;
- cross-institutional enrolment;
- choice in times of enrolment;
- methodologies that cater for a wider range of learners, learning styles, needs and interests;
- learners given greater responsibility for their learning;
- modular formats providing choice in the pace or order of studies, faculty contact, and times and forms of assessment;

- resource based learning, using various educational technologies

Open learning is used in developed and developing countries (Perraton, 2000), to increase the opportunities for, and improve the quality of, primary and secondary schooling, to provide 'second chance' non-formal adult and community education (Yates & Bradley, 2000), and for the purposes of vocational education and training (Calder & McCollum, 1998), teacher training (Perraton, 1996; Robinson & Latchem, in press) and higher education (Harry, 1999). In all countries and fields of human endeavour, knowledge and skills life-cycles are shortening, working and learning are becoming indivisible and there is need for lifelong and 'just-in-time' learning. Universities, colleges and other providers are recognizing the value and income-generating potential of open learning for professional and continuing education, and targeting major employers and professional associations capable of delivering hundreds of students in a single deal. Globalization, technology, competition and financial exigencies are leading to the transformation of existing institutions and the creation of new ones.

Two to three years ago, after reviewing global developments in open and distance education, Farrell (1999) and Cunningham et al. (2000) concluded that there was more rhetoric than reality in the concept of 'virtual education'. Today, Farrell (2001) concludes from current 'macro developments' that in terms of the rhetoric, open and flexible, virtual and e-learning now feature in the planning agendas and learning environments of most institutions, and in terms of reality, are increasingly adding value to the traditional delivery models.

Hanna (2000) identifies seven new or emerging organizational models of higher education: extended traditional universities; for-profit, adult-centred universities; distance education/technology-based universities; corporate universities; university-university and university-industry strategic alliances; degree/certification competency-based universities; and global multinational universities.

The *extended traditional universities* are all of those conventional institutions now moving from single-mode (on-campus) to dual-mode or providing their courses through some mix of on- and off-campus education. Examples of *for-profit, adult-centred universities* are the online University of Phoenix (*http://www.onl.uophx.edu/*) and accredited web-based Jones International University (http:jiu-web-a.jonesinternational.edu). The *distance education/technology-based universities* are the 'mega-universities' and other open universities (Daniel, 1996), of which the latest is Universitas Terbuka Malaysia (Unitem) (Wotjas, 2001). *Corporate universities,* which are essentially extended human resource organizations have established, for example, by American Express, Intel and Disney, but have not evolved to the extent originally envisaged. An example of a *university-university alliance* is the Virtual University of the Monterrey Institute of Technology which comprises universities within and beyond Mexico (*http://www.ruv.itesm.mx/*, and Scottish Knowledge, a consortium of fourteen Scottish universities and colleges. This consortium also includes corporate members, including News plc with twenty-five percent equity in this initiative. Other examples of *university-industry partnerships* include the 'virtual business school' established by the Henley Management College and UK management consultants Ernst & Young and the UK University for Industry (U*f*I) public-private initiative (*http://www.ufiltd.co.uk*) designed to provide a nationwide training network and improve economic competitiveness, work performance and employment prospects. It is not yet easy to identify a *degree/certification competency-based university.* However, one new provider type not identified by Hanna is *the broker*. Western Governors' University (*http://www.wgu.edu*), acts as a broker for competency-based undergraduate and graduate programmes provided by its member institutions, and Open Learning Australia (*http://www.ola.edu.au*) brokers entry and degree pathways for nontraditional students through its shareholding member universities and other institutions. Examples of *global multinational universities* or rather consortia, may be seen in the University of Melbourne-led Universitas21 consortium of universities in ten countries partnered with Thomson Learning (*http://ww.universitas21.com*), and a global consortium of twelve Australian Canadian, Dutch, New Zealand, UK and US universities partnered with Hong Kong-based educational and training company NextEd, aiming for the Asian higher education market.

By ignoring institutional, geographic and political inhibitors to growth, exploiting technology and providing flexible lifelong learning, institutions such as these are fundamentally challenging the traditional institution which, as Bates (1995) reminds us, was designed for economies and societies that are fast disappearing. Further changes are predicted.

Educational Technologies

Successive generations of open and distance educators have been equally quick to seize upon each new delivery system and service provider to extend and enrich the basic print/correspondence model—radio in the 1930s, television in the 1950s, audiotapes in the 1960s, videotapes and audioconferencing in the 1970s, and more recently, videoconferencing (particularly in the US and India), computers, CD-ROMs and the Internet/Web. However, there have been many unrealised expectations and 'false dawns' in introducing educational technologies. For example, UK Prime Minister Harold Wilson originally envisaged the Open University (OU) as 'the University of the Air'. In practice, while radio and television have been invaluable in recruiting learners and enriching learning, print and correspondence have until very recently formed the core of OU course delivery. Today, many claims are being made regarding the potential of 'e-learning' or 'virtual learning'.

Educational technologies can enhance access, make available the best of courses and tuition, provide faster interaction, reduce feelings of isolation and create learning communities, and help to make the learning 'more real' by providing examples in sound and vision. Used wisely, they can also offer considerable cost savings over traditional means of providing education and training, but they cannot of themselves empower those who lack the knowledge and skills to exploit them, nor can they guarantee successful learning outcomes. Much time and effort is needed to develop and deliver quality programmes and build learner awareness of, and competence in, technologies and their educational applications. Moreover, there are important equity issues to be borne in mind. Electronic delivery may be cheaper and more convenient for the providers and more speedy and reliable for the end users, but the connection costs or costs of printing out downloaded copy may be too high for some learners or they may lack the necessary network or computing capacity. There are also important human considerations. Asynchronous online interaction may suit those who can only log on for their learning at particular times, but the group dynamics are quite different from those of face-to-face teaching and learning and learners more familiar with the teacher-dependency of the traditional classroom or lacking the necessary motivation or self-direction may need considerable, and therefore costly, support and reassurance.

Many studies over the years have shown that no educational technology is inherently and universally better than any other. In open learning, what is needed is a carefully considered mix of face-to-face instruction, print, audiovisual, CD-ROM or Web based study material, and Web-based tools such as email, discussion groups/bulletin boards and chat rooms.

Educational technologies may be used to support virtually every aspect of open learning, for example:

- *Course outlines,* providing educational and administrative details, lecture notes, study guides and reading lists, may be delivered through print or electronic means.
- *Teaching material* and on-campus lectures can be delivered through print, audiocassette, videotape, CD-ROM, satellite or the Internet.
- *Independent and guided study material* can be provided

in print, online, CD-ROM or audiovisual learning packages.

- *Interactive lectures and seminars,* enabling learners to question and be questioned on their reading and assignments, can be provided via audioconferences, audiographics or videoconferences.
- *Assignment writing* can be facilitated by the drafting and re-drafting capabilities of the computer and word processing software.
- *Assignment delivery and feedback* can be speedily, cheaply and reliably achieved via the Web.
- *Tutorials and peer learning,* in which learners share their thoughts, experiences, findings, and concerns, can be provided through audioconferencing, text-based or video chat, electronic whiteboards (where there is need to share documents and graphics), computer conferencing, or videoconferencing.
- *Library and database searches* can be facilitated through CD-ROMs and the Web.
- *Library and inter-library loans* arranged through email.
- *Practical work and research* can be assisted by computer- and Internet-based simulations and case-based teaching and learning tools offering animation, hypertext, diagnostic networks, etc.

Sustaining Technology and Disruptive Technology

Christensen (2000) distinguishes between 'sustaining technology' and 'disruptive technology'. *Sustaining technology* progresses along an evolutionary line and enables established industries to improve their existing products. *Disruptive technology,* on the other hand, starts by offering markedly different benefits at lower cost, is initially rejected by the customers but succeeds in seeking out and serving new and emerging markets, improves with growing demand, achieves the quality expectations of the mainstream market, and finally displaces the established products, bringing about revolutionary change in the industry. Translating these concepts into educational technology, sustaining technology helps improve existing ways of teaching and learning, and disruptive technology changes the teaching learning environment.

The introduction of prepaid post (the Penny Black) in England in 1840 led Isaac Pitman to see the commercial potential of correspondence education. By so doing, he redefined mid-19th century education and training and stimulated the rapid spread of correspondence education, home study and the university extension movement throughout the UK, Europe and the US. During the second half of the 20th century, the tools and techniques of mass production, mass media and multimedia were employed again, not in the established markets, but to transform universities into 'dual-mode', create totally new institutions, the open universities, and offer academic, professional development and general programmes to a far wider public. Now the Internet/Web is leading to further transformations in institutional structures and practices and the creation of new alliances and 'virtual institutions' targeting global markets. What began at the 'low end' of the marketplace as correspondence education is becoming a dominant force, and tradition, bureaucracy, and skepticism about the potential of the technologies are now seen as stalling institutional progress.

Educational Technologies and Open Learning in Asia

So vigorously has Asia pursued alternative modes of delivery that the region can now claim an increasing number of universities moving into dual-mode, five of the world's ten 'mega-universities' (Daniel, 1996), the world's newest open university—Unitem, established by Malayasia's 11 public universities as a private company offering e-learning opportunities throughout southeast Asia (Wotjas, 2001)—and the world's largest enrolment in open and distance education (Capper, 1998). Notable gains in access and equity have been achieved by, for example, Indira Gandhi National Open University (Khan, 2001); Thailand's Sukhotai Thammathirat

Open University (Teswanitch, 1994);, the China Radio and Television Universities (Sun & Li, 1997; Ding, 1998); the Open University of Hong Kong; University of the Air of Japan (Iwanaga, 1994; Takahashi, 1997; University of the Air, 1998); the Korea National Open University (Kim & Hong, 1997; Jung & Leem, 1998); and the University of the Philippines Open University. Like Unitem, some Asian distance teaching universities, for example, Indira Gandhi National Open University and the Macau-based Asian International Open University are also internationalising their programmes, and UK, Australian, American and other distance teaching universities are expanding their operations and forming strategic alliances with institutions within the region (Cunningham et al., 1997).

Traditionally, Asian open and distance education has used some combination of print, classroom/study centre, broadcast/taped and correspondence instruction, but there is now increasing interest in using ICT. South Asia's largest distance education provider, IGNOU, is the only university in the world with its own educational TV channel, *Gyan Darshan*[7] (Knowledge Network) on the national *Doordarshan* (Television) network, and it also uses interactive television, computers and the internet to enhance access and learning through its telelearning centres and regional study centres. South Korea is experimenting with ICT and virtual learning (Jung, 1999). Singapore, which is already fully cabled for interactivity, has the highest per capita rate of Internet connection in the region and can claim usage patterns close to those of the US, is spending millions of dollars to reform its educational institutions and teaching methods. Malaysia also has ambitious plans to harness technology and open learning in pursuit of its '2020 vision' of 40 per cent of the population holding post-secondary qualifications by the second decade of the millennium

It is estimated that there are 104.88 million people in Asia

7. Editors' Note: Gyan Darshan is 24-hour national educational channel. It is hosted by IGNOU.

already online, which is about 25 per cent of those globally connected (see Table 1 below); the December 2000 'guesstimate' of the number of people online worldwide was 418.59 million (Nua Internet Surveys, 2001: *www.nua.ie/surveys/* how_many_online/asia.html). Connectivity is rising more quickly in Asia than in the West and the number of Internet users was predicted to double by 2002. Online applications are also increasing quickly: in September 2001, over 60 per cent of all China's Websites had been created in the previous eighteen months. However, for e-learning to become a reality across all parts of the Asian region, many more learners will need to be able to access, and afford, quality-assured wired, wireless or satellite portals to the global network, in their homes or workplaces, or in the more disadvantaged communities, through telephony and computer-based services provided in the form of public-access 'telecentres' or 'telecottages'. Many international and national development agencies are now helping to establish such centres in countries ranging from Ecuador to Bhutan, thus providing previously undreamed-of opportunities for teleeducation, teletraining, telemedicine,

Table 1: Internet Users in Asia in October 2001

Year of latest Survey	*Country users*	*No. of Internet*	*% of population*
1999	Bangladesh	30,000	0.02
1999	Bhutan	500	0.02
2000	China	16.9 m	1.34
1999	Brunei Daressalam	4,000	1.19
2000	Hong Kong	3.4 m	48.69
2000	India	4.5 mi	0.45
1999	Indonesia	0.4m	0.18
2000	Japan	38.64 m	30.53
1999	Kazakhstan	70,000	0.42
1999	Kyrgyzstan	10,000	0.21
1999	Malaysia	1.5 m	6.88
1999	Philippines	0.5m	0.62
2000	Singapore	1.85 m	44.58
2000	South Korea	16.4 m	34.55
1998	Sri Lanka	65,000	0.34
1999	Taiwan	6.4 m	28.84
2000	Thailand	1 m	1.65
1999	Vietnam	100,000	0.13

Source: *www.nua.ie/surveys/*how_many_online/asia.html

telecommerce and telework (Latchem & Walker, 2001), and in India, IGNOU is also leading the way by establishing its telelearning centres (Panda & Chaudhary, 2001)

There will undoubtedly be increasing pressure on Asia's educational institutions to embrace ICT, to increase access and equity, to reduce costs, to reach out into potentially lucrative markets, and to offset growing competition from private, offshore and virtual providers. However, in many countries across the region, particularly in rural and remote areas, the telecommunications infrastructure is inadequate, telephone density limits access to the Internet, access costs are high, and even where it is possible to provide PSTN (public switched telephone network), the faster PDN (public data network), or leased lines, it is still difficult to deliver 'over the last mile' to those very people in the villages and poor peri-urban or city neighbourhoods who are most in need of open learning.

Oestmann and Dymond (2001) point to the fact that in developed nations, the twin vehicles for accelerating telecommunications infrastructure development are privatization and competition. The former injects the much-needed capital for speedier network upgrades and rollouts that cash-strapped state-owned monopolies cannot afford and the latter drives down service costs. However, they acknowledge that some developing countries may find it politically difficult to fully liberalize their telecommunications, being fearful of undermining their national and regional development goals. Educational applications of the Internet may also be constrained by English not being the primary language of many learners, the limited amount of software capable of handling local languages, and the fact that domain names currently require Roman characters in their Web addresses.

Can ICT meet the needs of organisations and learners and provide robust, cost effective learning environments?

Determining the current costs (cost-efficiency), expected costs (cost-utility), quality and quantity of outcomes (cost effectiveness), and returns on investment (cost-benefit) of educational technologies and open learning and comparing these with the costs of conventional education is bedevilled by problems of definition, data collection, and interpretation. This leads to considerable subjectivity in costing and judging educational innovations. Nevertheless, despite all these difficulties, it is important for managers and practitioners to try to establish the long-term costs and resource implications of open and flexible learning and whether these are justified by the outcomes. Rumble & Oliveira (1992), Rumble (1987; 1999), Dhanarajan et al. (1994), Daniel (1996), and others show that distance education can be cheaper *per student* than comparable conventional education. However, it is also observed that dropout and repetition rates may be high in some mega- and open universities, so the *cost per graduate* may be far less impressive. In saying that distance education can be cheaper, Rumble (1999a) adds the important caveat—*under the right circumstances*. He agrees that large-scale technology-based distance teaching systems can be cost-efficient relative to *un-reformed* traditional systems, but questions whether they are necessarily so compared with *reformed* systems. Karelis (1999) records that while US universities find greater educational benefit in using 'distributed learning' than traditional lectures, they find it difficult to achieve similar returns on investment, let alone savings. He concludes that such returns would only be achievable if enrolments were to exceed significantly what was both possible and conducive to quality learning. The slowing rate of university experimentation in online or in virtual learning in the US which is reported almost weekly in the Chronicle of Higher Education suggests that the funding implications of such development is causing senior managers to more critically evaluate the benefits and costs to their organizations. As Carr (2001) observes: 'In fact, several distance education leaders predict that some administrators will slow or stop their expansion into online learning as they develop a better sense of the costs. And many college officials are at least trying to explore various assumptions about distance learning by focusing on costs.' Costing and sustainability studies are most important for any organization embarking on such mode of delivery.

It is really too early to provide firm answers to questions

of how much and what sort of ICT-enhanced/online teaching and learning is appropriate and viable for learners, staff and institutions. As with previous 'new technologies', the answers will lie in mix and the quality of these technologies and resources and their deployment. What we do know is that groups of staff and students react to these new opportunities/threats in varying ways.

The need is for staff and learners to re-conceptualise the learning process in the ICT environment. Staff also need to identify the *stances* they adopt towards this new learning environment, as this will impact both on their design preferences and tutoring activities. To help identify various university-based collective constructions of, and attitudes toward, Internet technology in literacy education, Bruce (1997: 290-291) developed a model of six stances: Neutrality, Opposition, Utilitarian, Skeptical, Transformational and Aesthetic. Fox & Herrmann (2000) have adapted and redefined four of Bruce's stances and created an additional stance, which more readily describes archetypal ways of thinking about online technology and its application. These five stances are: Neutralitarians, Boosters (see also Bigum and Kenway, 1998), Oppositionals, Skeptics and Transformationalists. Table 2 below describes the characteristics of these stances.

Table 2: Stances Towards Technology

Stances	*Characteristics*
Neutralitarian	Online technology makes no significant difference to student learning or course content. Technology does not change the learning process.
Boosters	The new online technologies will improve learning and make education in general more effective and efficient. New developments in technology are inherently good and non-problematic.
Oppositional	Technology simplifies and changes complex teaching and learning processes and practices. The danger is that ultimately, machines will take the place of teachers.
Skeptic	Sees a huge gap between the rhetoric and reality of technology application and practice.
Transformationalist	Technology radically changes content and processes

Source: Fox & Herrmann, 2001

It is important for change agents and staff developers to be able to differentiate between these stances in both staff and learners. In the case of staff, failure to do this will lead to dysfunctional e-learning provision or even non-compliance, and in the case of learners, a mis-matching of users and services (both under and over servicing) and higher attrition rates.

It is also important to consider how the twin drivers of cost efficiency and quality impact on the deployment of ICT in open learning. Systemic and institutional issues have already been addressed above, but we also need to analyse the impact at the level of deployment. Bates (2000) describes the tendency for staff to adopt a 'lone ranger' approach to technology development in open learning. The desire of some teachers to develop their own resources has also been debated by, e.g. Renner (1995) and Campion (1995). The underlying premise is that the introduction of the 'new media' or ICT empowers staff and students to take control of the learning process and progress from the 'Fordist' (industrial or mass produced) model employed by the large print-based open and distance universities. However, from organizational and funding perspectives, for e-learning process and outcomes to be successful, issues of consistency, coherence and quality in the learning and technological environments must be assured if undesirable or unintended outcomes are to be avoided (Herrmann et al. 2000). The isolationist or 'cottage industry' approach to course and instructional design militates against such centralized intervention and prevents the sharing and multiple usage of (Web-based) resources. For educational applications of the Web to be pedagogically successful and financially viable, it is important to avoid the creation or maintenance of isolated, single-purpose teaching sites across educational/training institutions or systems. The cost of maintenance and version control can add enormously to the budget.

Learners' perceptions, expectations and experiences are highly diverse, and for all the rhetoric about the need for the market to be 'demand driven' rather than 'supply driven', there is a danger that in the drive for cost efficiency or market domination, open learning will be 'commodified' rather than designed for the needs of individual learners. The current move to database driven teaching sites provides a potentially cost effective and pedagogically sound approach to e-learning. Here, rather than creating static and specific Web pages based purely on content and linked to form a teaching site, an outcomes based approach is adopted. Once the course outcomes have been identified, the content is structured in concepts, and components of these concepts are developed as 'learning objects'. At its simplest level, a learning (or knowledge) object is a discrete or self-contained piece of information of instruction designed to be viewed on the Web. It may be as small as a single Web page containing a few lines of text, an image, an animation, or a movie clip.

For teaching staff and instructional designers, this concept of learning objects requires a fundamental change in thinking. Instead of the teaching process being viewed as a linear sequence with a defined beginning, middle and end, the learning objects are viewed as clustered sets comprising independent, standalone elements of information and learning, some of which may be interrelated at one level of understanding and therefore viewed as a single group, but all of which may also be accessed as discrete, unconnected entities. The key to effectively deploying learning objects is to provide ways of enabling the learner to contextualise the information and select appropriate objects according to need. Without this, learning objects can be confusing, misleading, or meaningless (Quinton, 2001; Daniel 2001). Such an approach to instructional design addresses the apparent paradox of customizing courses to meet individual needs while providing programmes cost effectively for mass, online education, and suggests the way forward for online/open learning. Regardless of the developmental environment and tools used, sound instructional design is essential both for customized development and template-based development. The combination of thoughtful planning with intelligent deployment of advanced authoring tools will result in a multitude of benefits for both content designers and learners.

The question of the status of distance and open learning was addressed earlier but may also reflect changes in the way in which learners perceive university study and learning in general. McInnis (2001: *http://www.cshe.unimelb.edu.au/downloads/InaugLec23_8_01.pdf*) states that in Australia, students are increasingly disengaging, not only from the greater use of more flexible modes of teaching and learning, but higher education studies in general. He suggests that: 'We have to ask if we are judging the nature and extent of student engagement by standards and measures that are no longer appropriate. Trying to recreate the campus-based experience from a distance may be seriously distracting from the potential of new technologies. While there may be far more to the effective undergraduate experience than instruction, to achieve these outcomes in the face of negotiated engagement means that the social dimensions of the campus-based experience will have to be managed with considerably more skill and resources than in the past. These experiences will not happen without intervention as might have been the case when small numbers of students studied and played their way through courses together.' (p9) He goes on to underline that less time on campus does not reduce the need for support but changes the nature of the support that is needed. Many writers now observe that there is a 'blurring' of the distinction between on- and off-campus education, and this is not necessarily productive or inherently beneficial to the students as it may mean that all students are treated and supported in the same way to the disadvantage of the off-campus student who in dual-mode institutions, is all too often either marginalized or only thought of in the context of the mainstream population.

Given these considerations, it may well be that the use of such terms as 'virtual classroom' and 'virtual university' are counterproductive in that they imply that the experience of the ICT learning environment is always the same as that of face-to-face teaching and learning. It suggests that all of the cultural, social and psychological baggage and counterproductive power relations and attitudes of the traditional classroom or university are to be maintained. These are also terms that can be used pejoratively, suggesting that they are less than 'real'. New forms of teaching and learning must be removed from old mindsets if they are to achieve their true potency.

Future Trends and Needs

Faced with the need for economy in upgrading the knowledge and skills of their populations, sometimes over great distances, and for quality in educational content and delivery, governments seem likely to seek solutions in open learning. Daniel (1996) observes that by increasing university capacity dramatically while lowering costs sharply, the single mode open universities, and particularly those he calls the 'mega-universities' with enrolments of over 100,000, represent a rare discontinuity in the evolution of higher education. They will undoubtedly play a key role in changing perceptions of what is possible in educational provision. The shift from a 'supply-driven' to a 'demand-driven' educational market presents a serious challenge to the values and practices of the traditional universities and colleges. They will need to become more open and flexible in their approaches, entrepreneurial in seeking out new markets, quality conscious in the face of competition and sensitive to the needs of their non-traditional constituency of off-campus, part-time, working adults.

Open learning may at first only be a marginal activity in some of the more conventional institutions, embraced by a few and seen as threatening time honoured roles, practices and standards by the majority. However, the growing demand for access, convenience and flexibility and the increasing recognition of the commercial potential of distance education approaches will undoubtedly strengthen institutional commitment, and the new forms of course development and delivery will influence the curriculum. The increasing use of ICT will blur distinctions between on- and off-campus teaching and learning, and the different types of student and funding bases will lead to a re-framing of institutional missions and operations and the emergence of new organizational models.

US brokerage house Merrill-Lynch estimates global

expenditure on education and training to be $US2 trillion, 50 per cent of which is in Europe, 33 per cent in the US and 15 per cent in developing countries. The potential global market for online learning is attracting new for-profit providers that may present formidable competition to any traditional institution incapable of change. They aim to maximize profits for their shareholders by focusing on the more profitable subject areas such as business and information technology, minimising investment in physical plant and student services, and not committing resources to research or community activities. Their course development, teaching and assessment may be carried out by different people, in-house or outsourced. They design their courses to appeal to large numbers of students in multiple locations, and in such ways that they completed in shorter time through year-round part-time study, thus minimizing loss of income by the students. As discussed above, consortia or strategic alliances, some international, are also being created in order to capture member institutions' primary strengths, compete against potential rivals or interlopers, and overcome hurdles of language, culture, accreditation, articulation and student support in educational 'export'. The growing market for professional degrees and short courses is also leading to new ventures between universities (providing the 'brand names', intellectual property, pedagogy, credentials and credibility) and commercial publishers or multimedia companies (providing the business and marketing expertise and technology that enables the universities to profit from their endeavours). These consortia are eyeing global markets and could turn out to be highly profitable enterprises. The main challenges they face are cultural conflicts between academia and industry, and how to ensure agreement on inter-institutional and worldwide quality assurance systems and accreditation (Cunningham et al., 1997). Daniel (1999) warns of the 'imperial fantasies' of these alternative providers and the danger of their skimming off the cream of undergraduate and professional programmes provided by the public institutions.

It seems almost inevitable that technology will lead

universities and colleges to become 'clicks and mortar' institutions, some focusing on national or regional markets, others with a more international focus. Chipman (1999) predicts that within twenty years, all universities will be universal or nearly so, entered and re-entered at multiple points in people's lives, international in focus and delivery, and robust in their quality standards. He suggests that institutions will receive nothing like the current levels of taxpayer support, and will need to organize their programmes to meet rising student expectations of convenient delivery, reduce their input costs per graduate, become more competitive, and shed time-honoured assumptions and practices.

The Challenges for Asian Institutions

In planning for the future of open learning in Asia, it is important to heed Ramanujam (1997), who warns of introducing western models of open learning into developing countries where these may be neither fully understood nor in accord with the traditional values and practices of the educators or society at large and Koul (1998), who observes that some politicians and planners are carried away by success stories of open learning and totally underestimate the problems of thrusting self-directed learning upon staff and learners conditioned by the traditional classroom.

Bates (1995) argues that our traditional educational institutions were basically designed for the educational needs of societies and economies that are fast disappearing and that we need new organizational systems to support flexible lifelong learning and exploit educational technologies. He sees challenges ahead, both for the dedicated single mode open learning institutions, which being designed to meet unserved mass markets, find it easier to offer homogeneous products than customize their offerings, and the conventional institutions, which find it difficult to move beyond a 'lone ranger' approach to innovation and be fast to market with new courses (Bates, 1999; 2000).

There have been some great achievements in using

educational technologies. But there are also many instances of 'technological determinism'—institutions seeing ICT as providing a 'quick fix' solution to their problems and focusing on 'digital products' rather than learners' needs.

Staff cannot be expected to venture into open and online learning without training, recognition and reward. McInnis (2001) found that 66 per cent of staff in Australian universities was engaged in developing ICT courseware, 72 per cent with computer-based learning, and 46 per cent in distance education. Two-thirds reported that this work was having a major impact on their teaching and accounted for half their working week. Their main motivations were the availability of the technology, university policies and student expectations. However, few received any formal training for this work and many complained that when it came to promotions, educational development counted for less than research.

Chattell (1995) suggests that there is a danger that the commercialisation of open learning and pressures to recruit more students will lead to the learner being seen as no more an economic target to be captured. It is vitally important to bear in mind that all learners have highly differentiated needs and preferences and that, as Farrell (1999) observes, the educational market is fragmenting into niche markets. Internet marketing experts stress the importance of viewing the Internet, not as a market of 100 million, but as 100 million markets. So, rather than 'commodifying' open learning in pursuit of cost efficiency or market domination, there is need to develop 'learning objects' or personalized modules of learning.

The best of the institutions involved in open learning are leading the way in using technology to provide access, equity, and student-centred lifelong learning. They recognise that they are now operating in an economic climate in which they are expected to achieve more with less, generate a greater percentage of their income, and evidence the costs, quality and cost benefits of what they offer. They are also operating in a technological environment which holds great promise. It is important that they continue to democratise education and guard against the creation of two systems—one of high standing for those who are able to afford the study costs and the technology; the other providing inferior services and qualifications for the socio-economically and geographically disadvantaged. They must also ensure that their strategies and performance are strong enough to compete against those hungry for greater market share.

To cope with the financial realities and competitiveness of the 21st century, institutions need to become more entrepreneurial. They need to be run, not by mere managers, but by transformational leaders (Latchem & Hanna, 2001). There must be considerable investment in human as well as technological resources (Latchem & Lockwood, 1998). There is also a need to continually question, and improve upon, institutional policies, procedures, and outcomes. To achieve all of these may not always be easy in Asian contexts, but Asian problems need Asian answers.

An Afterword

At the start of this chapter we described Tagore's vision for open learning in India and how this was not realized within his lifetime. But that is not the end of the story. The English social entrepreneur Leonard Elmhirst, who once worked as secretary to Tagore and was strongly influenced by his thinking, many years later applied his radical ideas on education in founding Dartington Hall in England. One of Dartington's ex-pupils, similarly imbued with these ideas for optimizing human learning, was Michael (now Lord) Young, who in 1962 proposed an open university for the UK and established the National Extension College as a pilot for such an initiative (Perraton, 1999). The visions of leaders may not always be immediately realized, but can take root and benefit generations of learners. The greatest challenge is to identify and nurture such leadership at every level of the educational and training system.

REFERENCES

Bates, A.W. (1995) *Technology: Open Learning and Distance Education*, Routledge, London & New York.

Bates, A.W. (1999) 'Are open universities dead?', keynote address, the 13th Annual Conference of the Asian Association of Open Universities, *Open and Distance Education Systems and Models Facing 21st Century's Information and Learning Societies*, October 14-17, Beijing, China.

Bates, A.W. (2000) *Managing Technological Change: Strategies for College and University Leaders*, Jossey-Bass, San Francisco.

Bigum, C. and Kenway, J. (1998) New information technologies and the ambiguous future of schooling: some possible scenarios, in A. Hargreaves, A. Lieberman, M. Fullan, and D. Hopkins (eds.) *International Handbook of Educational Change*, pp 375-395, Kluwer Academic Publishers, Dordrecht.

Boshier, R.W. & Pratt, D. (1997). A qualitative and postmodern perspective on open learning in Hong Kong. *Distance Education, 18* (1), pp. 110-135.

Bruce, B.C. (1997) Critical issues. Literacy Technologies: What Stance Should We Take? *Journal of Literacy Research*, 29(2), pp. 269-309

Calder, J. & McCollum, A. (1998) *Open and Flexible Learning in Vocational Education and Training*, Kogan Page, London.

Campion, M. (1995) The supposed demise of bureaucracy: Implications for distance education and open learning—more on the post-Fordist debate. *Distance Education*, 16, (2), pp. 192—216.

Capper, J. (1998) Distance education in uncertain times. Keynote address at the Asian Association of Open Universities 12th Annual Conference *The Asian Distance Learner*, November 4-6, The Open University of Hong Kong, Hong Kong, SAR, China.

Carr, S. (2001) Is Anyone Making Money on Distance Education? *Chronicle of Higher Education*, February 16.

Chattell, A. (1995) *Managing For the Future*, Macmillan Business, Basingstoke & London.

Cheng, K-M. (1998) International collaboration in higher education: Challenges of the Information Era, plenary address at the 12th Association of Asian Open Universities, Conference, *The Asian Distance Learner*, 4-6 November, 1998, The Open University of Hong Kong.

Cheng, K-M., Jin, X. & Gu, X. (1998) Challenging state planning: Adult higher education in China, in *Comparative Education*, 34(4).

Chipman, L (1999) 'Welcome to Lifetime Learning Inc', *The Australian: Higher Education*, September 8, p. 44 (edited version of a paper

'Visioning Our Future' delivered to the Central Queensland University Council).

Christensen, C.M. (2000) The Innovator's Dilemma. (Harperbusiness, New York).

Cunningham, S., Tapsall, S., Ryan, Y., Stedman, L., Bagdon, K. & Flew, T. (1997) *New Media and Borderless Education: A Review of the Convergence Between Global Media Networks and Higher Education Provision*, Evaluations and Investigations Program, Higher Education Division, Department of Employment, Education, Training and Youth Affairs, Australian Government Publishing Service, Canberra, ACT.

Cunningham, S., Ryan, Y., Stedman, L., Tapsall, S., Bagdon, K., Flew, T. & Coaldrake, P. (2000) *The Business of Borderless Education*, Evaluations and Investigations Program, Higher Education Division, Department of Education, Training and Youth Affairs, Australian Government Publishing Service, Canberra, ACT.

Daniel, J.S. (1996) Mega-universities and Knowledge Media: Technology Strategies for Higher Education, Kogan Page, London.

Daniel, J.S. (1999) 'Distance learning in the era of networks,' *The ACU Bulletin of Current Documentation*, 138 (April), pp. 7-9.

Daniel, D. (2001) Most learning objects aren't. *http://www.nyuonline.com/vn_3/inside/articles/objects_aren't.html* accessed 7th September, 2001.

Dede, C. (2000) 'Advanced technologies and distributed learning in higher education', In D.E. Hanna & Associates (eds.) *Higher Education in an Era of Digital Competition: Choices and Challenges*, Atwood Publishers, Madison, WI, pp. 71-91

Dhanarajan, G, Ip, P K, Yuen, K S & Swales, C (1994) *Economics of Distance Education: Recent Experience*, Open Learning Institute Press, Open Learning Institute of Hong Kong.

Ding, X. (1998). Evaluation of distance teaching universities: Chinese perspectives and experiences, Keynote address at *The International Open and Distance Education Symposium*, April 15-17, Shanghai Television University, Shanghai, China.

Farrell, G (ed.) (1999) *The Development of Virtual Education: A Global Perspective*, The Commonwealth of Learning, *http://www.col.org/virtualed/index.htm*

Farrell, G. (ed.) (2001) *The Changing Faces of Virtual Education*, The Commonwealth of Learning, http://www.col.org/virtualed/index2.htm

Fox, R. & Herrmann, A. (2000) 'Changing media, changing times: Coping with adopting new educational technologies, in T. Evans & D. Nation (eds.) *Changing University Teaching: Reflections on Creating Educational Technologies*, Kogan Page, London.

Hanna, D.E. (2000) 'Emerging organizational models: The extended traditional university', in D E Hanna & Associates (eds.) *Higher Education in an Era of Digital Competition: Choices and Challenges*, Atwood Publishers, Madison, WI, pp. 93-116.

Harry, K. (ed.) (1999) *Higher Education Through Open and Distance Learning*, Routledge, London.

Herrmann, A., Fox, R. & Boyd, A. (2000) 'Unintended effects in using learning technologies', in E. Burge (ed), *The Strategic Use of Learning Technologies.* New Directions for Adult and Continuing Education, No. 80, San Francisco.

Iwanaga, M. (1994) 'Elderly students learning through the University of the Air system in Japan', *Educational Gerontology (2)*, pp. 473-482.

Johnson, R. (1990). *Open Learning: Policy and Practice.* National Board of Employment Education and Training Commissioned Report No. 4. Australian Government Publishing Service, Canberra, ACT.

Jones, G.R. (2001) 'Jones International University: Converging Marketplace Entrepreneurship and Education', in C. Latchem & D. Hanna (eds.) *Leadership for 21st Century Learning: Global Perspectives from Leading Innovators,* Kogan Page, London, pp. 225-234.

Jung, I (1999) 'The development of virtual institutions in Korea', Appendix 9.1 to Robert Shaw, M 'Virtual institutions in east and southeast Asia', in G. Farrell (ed) *The Development of Virtual Education: A global perspective*, The Commonwealth of Learning http://www.col.org/virtualed/index.htm

Jung, I. & Leem, J. (1998) 'Design strategies for developing Web-based training courses in a Korean context', in Conference Papers Part II (surnames H-L), Asian Association of Open Universities 12th Annual Conference *The Asian Distance Learner*, November 4-6, The Open University of Hong Kong, Hong Kong SAR, China, pp. 218-226.

Karelis, C (1999) *Educational technology and cost control: Four models*, Fund for the Improvement of Postsecondary Education, http://www.ed.gov/offices/OPE/FIPSE/LAAP/reading.html

Khan, A. (2001) 'Indira Gandhi National Open University and the Distance Education Council: Institution and System Building in India', in C. Latchem & D. Hanna (eds.) *Leadership for 21st Century Learning: Global Perspectives from Leading Innovators,* Kogan Page, London, pp. 147-156.

Kim, J.W. & Hong, S.J. (1997). Alternative approach to the educational quality assurance model for KNOU. Proceedings of Asian Association of Open Universities 11th Annual Conference *Quality Assurance and Distance and Open Learning: Volume 1*, November 11—14, Kuala Lumpur, Malaysia, pp. 130-138.

Koul, B. (1998). Pro-active staff development: The Indira Gandhi National Open University experience, in C. Latchem & F. Lockwood (eds.)

Staff Development in Open and Flexible Learning, Routledge, London, pp. 75-84.

Latchem, C. & Hanna, D. (2001) *Leadership for 21st Century Learning: Global Perspectives from Leading Innovators*, Kogan Page, London.

Latchem, C. & Lockwood, F. (eds.) (1998) *Staff Development in Open and Flexible Learning*, Routledge, London.

Latchem, C. & Walker, D. (2001) *Multi-purpose Community-based Telecentres*, The Commonwealth of Learning, Vancouver.

Liu, H.F. (1996) *Keju: Kaoshi de jiaoyu shijiao (Civil Examinations: Education Perspectives on Examination)*, Hubei Educational Publishers, Wuhan, China.

McInnis, C. (2001) *The Work Roles of Academics in Australian Universities*, Evaluations and Investigations Program, Higher Education Division, Department of Employment, Training and Youth Affairs, Canberra, ACT (*www.detya.gov.au/archive/highered/eippubs/*eip00_5)

McInnis, C. (2001) Signs of disengagement? The changing undergraduate experience in Australian Universities. Inaugural Professorial Lecture (13 August, 2001), Centre for the Study of Higher Education, University of Melbourne, Melbourne *http://www.cshe.unimelb.edu.au/downloads/InaugLec23_8_01.pdf*), accessed September 5, 2001.

Mukherjee, N. (1997). Lok Siksha Samsad (Council for People's Education). *Open Praxis, 2*, pp. 13 and 21.

ODLAA Times (1999) 7(3), Open and Distance Learning Association of Australia, Canberra, August, p 6.

Oestmann, S & Dymond, A.C. (2001) 'Telecentres—Experiences, Lessons and Trends', in C. Latchem & D. Walker (eds.) *Telecentres: Case Studies and Key Issues*, The Commonwealth of Learning, Vancouver, www.col.org/telecentres

Panda, S. & Chaudhary, S. (2001) 'Telelearning and Telelearning Centres in India' in C. Latchem & D. Walker (eds.) *Telecentres: Case Studies and Key Issues*, The Commonwealth of Learning, Vancouver, www.col.org/telecentres

Perraton, H. (1993) *Distance Education for Teacher Training*, Routledge, London,

Perraton, H. (1999) personal email to Colin Latchem.

Perraton, H. (2000) *Open and Distance Learning in the Developing World*, Routledge, London and New York.

Quinton, S. (2001) *Learning Theory in the Context of Recent Technologies*, Unpublished Doctoral Thesis, University of Western Australia, Perth.

Ramanujam, P.R. (1997). 'Distance education in the 21st century: Implications for developing countries', in CD-ROM Conference Papers of *The New Learning Environment: A Global Perspective*, the 18th ICDE World Conference, Pennsylvania State University: USA, June 2-6.

Ren, F. (1998) 'On Higher Education Examinations for Self-taught Learners and strategies for their reform and development', in proceedings of the 22nd Annual International Association of Educational Assessment Conference, *The Effects and Related Problems of Large Scale Testing in Educational Assessment*, National Education Examinations Authority of China, Beijing, 20-25 September, 1996, Beijing, Foreign Language Teaching and Research Press of China, pp. 88-94.

Renner, W. (1995) Post-Fordist visions and technological solutions: Educational technology and the labour process, *Distance Education*, 16 (2), pp. 284-301.

Robinson, B. & Latchem, C. (in press) *Open and Distance Learning for Teacher Education*,

Volume 4, World Review of Distance Education and Open Learning, Routledge, London & New York/The Commonwealth of Learning, Vancouver.

Rumble G. (1997) *The Costs and Economics of Open and Distance Learning*, Kogan Page, London.

Rumble, G (1999) 'Cost analysis of distance learning', *Performance Improvement Quarterly*, 12 (2), pp 122-137.

Rumble, G & Oliveira, J-B (eds.) (1992) *Vocational Education at a Distance: International Perspectives*, International Labor Office/Kogan Page, London.

Rumble, G. & Latchem, C. (in press) 'Organisational models for open learning', in H. Perraton (ed.) *Policy for Open and Distance Learning*, Volume 3, World Review of Distance Education and Open Learning, Routledge, London & Mew York/Commonwealth of Learning, Vancouver.

Sun, L.Y. & Li, G.B. (Eds.) (1997). *1996 Education statistics yearbook of Radio and Television Universities in China*, China Central Television University Publishing House, Beijing, China.

Takashi, K. (1997) 'What do students really want of the University of the Air?', in proceedings of the 11th Asian Association of Open Universities Conference, *Quality Assurance in Distance & Open Learning: Volume* 2, November 11-14, Kuala Lumpur: Malaysia, pp. 298-301.

Teswanitch, J. (1994) 'Educational investment for distance education: Inequality that needs to be changed', in G. Dhanarajan, P.K. Ip, K.S. Yuen & C. Swales (eds.) *Economics of Distance Education: Recent Experience*, Open Learning Institute Press, Hong Kong SAR, China, pp. 42-57.

Turoff, M (1997) 'Costs for the development of a virtual university', *Journal of Asynchronous Learning*, 1(1) http://www.aln.org/alnWeb/journal/jaln_Vol1issue1.htm

University of the Air 1998 (1998) *The University of the Air*, Chiba, Japan.

Wotjas, O. (2001) 'Malaysian OU opts for Heriot-Watt expertise', in *The Times Higher*, August 3, p. 12.

Yates, C & Bradley, J (eds.) (2000) *Basic Education at a Distance*, Routledge, London and New York.

8

Strategies for Evaluating Technology in Education and Training

WELLESLEY R. FOSHAY* and D. WILLIAM QUINN**

In a generation, educational technology evaluation has matured from the "gee whiz!" stage (focused on what we can make the technology do) through the "does it work?" phase (focused on proving that it is possible to learn from technology), and now to "what's it good for?" phase (focused on each technology's relative strengths and weaknesses). Evaluation strategies in common use, however, are inadequate to the task. The most commonly-used strategies for evaluating technology apply experimental methods, or focus on cost comparisons. These strategies are often mis-applied, but more importantly, they often are based on assumptions which are inappropriate to the educational purpose of the technology, and fail to identify important effects. Thus, they often cannot answer the "what's it good for?" questions which are so critical to large-scale adoption.

This chapter has three parts. We will first examine the question of what effects of technology we can evaluate. Then we will present three basic evaluation strategies and discuss their application to technology. Finally, we will provide an overview of eight basic measurement strategies of use in technology evaluations.

---

*PLATO Learning, Inc., Bloomington, USA, **Quinn Evaluation, USA

What Should We Evaluate?

The evaluation of impact educational technology[8] by comparison of test scores in classes which do and do not use technology is usually done under conditions which make it impossible to attribute any results, whether desirable or undesirable, to the use of technology (or anything else). An evaluation based on a simple comparison of post-test scores (whether comparing two groups or a "before and after" or time series comparison) usually will fail to reveal the effects of technology, or will grossly underestimate them.

This is a matter of no small consequence. National policy initiatives to support technology are under way in many countries, and many of the policies wisely include a requirement for research-based evidence of effectiveness. However, in the U.S., as an example, the criteria for acceptable research-based evidence appear to emerge from the principle that just such experimental or quasi-experimental comparison studies should be the only evidence considered "rigorous." This is a posture educational technology policy-makers would do well to avoid. It also is inconsistent with current thinking on evaluation methodology, especially when applied to technology (Heinecke, Blasi, Milman and Washington, 1999). Furthermore, restricting the range of inquiry in this way will lead to the erroneous conclusion.

To see why simple comparison studies usually are of little use in evaluating technology, we should first examine what we know about its effects, and the reasons educators may choose to use technology.

8. "Technology" is often used today as a synonym for "computers" in the educational context. However, in this chapter we will use the term to apply to any of a broad class of mechanical devices and defined methods for their use in teaching and learning. There are many technologies in a conventional classroom, the oldest of which is the book. When a point refers exclusively to computers, we will say so.

What are the Effects of Technology?

It may seem counter-intuitive, but improvement of learning outcomes is only one of five basic reasons to use educational technology. The five reasons are to improve:

- learning outcomes
- instructional processes
- access
- cost
- organizational capability

To formulate an appropriate evaluation question, it is important to understand which of the five basic reasons, separately or in combination, are providing the motivation for a given project. We will examine each of them.

Effects on Learning Outcomes

Reviews of research on the effects of various media to classroom instruction and to each other for a generation (see Clark, 2000) commonly discard more than half of the studies reported because methodological limitations make the comparison uninterpretable. Attention to the sound studies, however, has led Clark and others to conclude that the apparent effects of technology are really attributable to superior instructional design. Clark has concluded that expecting technology to improve learning is like expecting a bakery delivery truck to improve the quality of the bread it carries. Honey, Culp and Carrigg (2000, p.2) came to a similar conclusion: "technologies by themselves have little scaleable or sustained impact on learning in schools." We concur that there are probably few effects on learning from technology as such, and simply introducing computers or any other technology into the classroom is likely to lead to few effects. Whatever differences are observed are likely to be due to subtle changes in instructional message design, including the quality and frequency of representations, responses and feedback. It makes little sense to attempt a similar generalization when evaluating technology's effects.

A Typology of Educational Software and their Uses

Evaluating various instructional designs requires us to consider what are the various uses of instructional technology. Within each of the uses, a number of instructional designs are possible, and they may be compared with some success. However, comparing one use to another probably does not make sense, because the intent of the software (and thus of the learning outcomes) differs. They can be *Supplementary* paralleling teaching already done in other modes; *Complementary* that adds new content to the curriculum, often in ways for which there is no non-computer alternative; and *Primary* that is the main source of initial teaching. A given software product (such as the PLATO Learning System) can often be used in more than one of the three ways, so notice that these definitions characterize the *way* in which software is used as much as *how* the software is designed.

An evaluation plan may use an externally-defined test, such as a standardized test keyed to curriculum standards. The test can be expected to measure the effects of software with defined learning outcomes, but it may well miss the effects of software with less-well defined outcomes, such as information and tools. Thus, an evaluation plan which relies solely on standardized test data may systematically ignore the learning outcomes produced by some classes of educational software.

An additional issue concerns the scale of use. A naïve error in evaluation of technology is to expect results on an end-of-semester or end-of-year cumulative test, when the technology use was confined to just a small percentage of learning time. A final consideration is: a comparison evaluation design is capable of detecting only net new additions to the curriculum, or net gains in learning of a common curriculum. There is, however, a corollary: technology uses which have ill-defined learning outcomes, or which are small in scale, or which are redundant to other teaching/learning activities, may not show major learning outcome gains when measured by the usual summative and cumulative end-of-semester or end-of-year test.

Effects on Process

In any learning environment, certain processes are valued particularly because they are believed to be closely associated with important curriculum objectives. For example, many educators believe that it is important to teach their students to be self-sufficient learners (McCombs, 2000) empowering students to question, seek information, initiate their own learning tasks and judge the results obtained. In this case, the technology evaluation should examine evidence of self-sufficient learning by the participating students independent of any cognitive learning measures.

Most well-planned education and training curricula use a portfolio of assessment techniques, which may include work products, observations of task performance, tests, oral performance, and other data. Since many of these data are often the most important measures of problem solving, thinking skills, and other higher-order learning outcomes which are the intended products of many uses of technology, it is important to give them appropriate weight in the technology evaluation. They will support conclusions about learning outcomes such as problem solving processes, and other indicators of thinking skills. The values of an education or training environment often define learning outcomes relating to goals such as initiative, persistence, citizenship, teamwork and character. Foshay (2000) defined the emotional, the social, the aesthetic, the physical and the spiritual domains, in addition to the cognitive. For him, defining the curriculum solely in terms of the cognitive domain is literally to deprive it of its humanity. Excellent teachers do many things in a classroom which are intended to convey lessons in these domains beyond the cognitive. A teacher who shows her enthusiasm for her subject is teaching important social and emotional lessons.

In PLATO evaluations, one of the most common observations is that learners feel successful in learning, whether or not they have a history of success in school learning. Process indicators such as these often can reveal much about the attractiveness, acceptability and "user friendliness" of educational software. Peer teaching and collaborative work on problem solving are an important part of PLATO's design, and can be observed in the classroom. Taken to its logical extension, effects on process can lead to an argument that the goal of technology is to produce a different *kind* of learning experience, with different goals, than those which are feasible by conventional classroom methods.

Effects on Access

Many educational technology implementations have as their primary goal improved access to learning by some defined population of learners. This goal is quite independent of learning outcomes. Examples of such implementations include distance learning initiatives designed to reach rural or home-bound students, continuing education programs, and programs designed for countries which face a shortage of qualified teachers. Some applications of technology are designed to improve mutual access of learners and instructors by creating online communities. Finally, some technology applications (particularly in corporate settings) seek to embed learning and knowledge management technologies directly in the work environment, thus bypassing much formal classroom training.

Distance Education. In secondary and post-secondary education, it is often tacitly assumed that the goal of distance education methods is to recreate the classroom experience in an on-line environment for whom campus-based learning is an undesirable option. A further complexity surrounds the structure of the distance education solution. Some distance solutions are purely on-line, but some have recognized that online and classroom methods are complementary, and a variety of mixed models of instruction are in use. This renders the technology-vs.-classroom comparison strategy even less applicable. In most cases, we conclude, evaluations of distance education programs should evaluate the entire program.

Learning Communities. Another way computers are used to improve access is by creation of online communities even when the participants are dispersed. Often the intent is to recreate the collegiality of classroom or small group interaction, while "breaking down the walls of the classroom" by making it possible for collaborative groups to operate over separations of space and time. The most basic criterion for evaluating learning communities is to examine participation, to see if the goal of access has been realized. Beyond this basic measure, it may make sense to evaluate the quality of interaction in the online community. This is especially the case if particularly desirable processes can be identified.

Just-in-time learning, performance support, and knowledge management. Another popular application of computers to improve access is to embed directly into the work environment activities and tools which facilitate learning, work, and the capture and dissemination of new knowledge (Rosenberg, 2000). The goal is to make new knowledge instantly available to all who need it, without the costs and delays of conventional training and education. These methods have a major influence in corporate environments, but in principle they could find application in education. For evaluating whether the goal of access has been achieved simple utilization statistics are of use. Evaluation of technology might first focus on utilization patterns, to determine if the goal of improved access to knowledge and skill has been met. Process measures might focus on analysis of interactions in a range of case problems. Performance measures might include sales figures, customer satisfaction, and perhaps additional key process measures such as time to develop proposals, competitive loss analysis, and the like.

Effects on Cost

Cost reduction without seeking particular improvement in learning outcomes is perhaps the most common motive behind e-Learning in corporate contexts. It is less common in education because most educational organizations have no way to offset the fixed costs of conventional instruction by use of technology-based delivery. However, cost analysis should be part of almost any major program evaluation, especially when technology is involved. The goal of cost analysis is to help to design programs that give greater value for the investment. In addition to being of great interest to decision makers and other constituents, cost analysis information is useful to program developers and operators. In fact, cost analysis is probably most valuable when used as a *formative* development tool, early in the implementation cycle.

Decision makers and other constituents are asking, "What is the return on the investment (ROI) made in technology-based systems?" Answering this questions means considering the issue of money as well as program effects (Lloyd, 1989). Gauging monetary effects of technology-based training beyond savings in delivery cost is often difficult. However, it may be possible to define the benefits of technology in terms of attainment of improved organizational capability (described below) to achieve strategic objectives. Obviously, this approach requires careful strategic planning, and alignment of technology applications to the strategic plan.

Any organization must have a plan for how it intends to achieve an improved "bottom line." Typically, these plans include a wide range of performance-based goals which are not directly measured on the "bottom line." Typical examples of such goals include improved customer service, improved product quality, reduced overhead, reduced time to market or cycle time, greater innovation, and the like. In an effective strategic planning process, these goals add up to the collective opinion of management about how the organization needs to improve in order to better its "bottom line."

For example, in PLATO Learning, Inc., the majority of new revenue comes from repeat business. Thus, client satisfaction is perceived as having a direct relationship to revenue, and thus to the "bottom line". In this case, the cost-benefit comparison includes a financial model on the "cost" side, but non-financial measures of client satisfaction on the "benefit" side. Conversely, if an action saves money but reduces customer satisfaction, then the cost is stated in non-financial measures, and the benefit is stated financially. This example brings to the surface the need to get the time frame right. It is often the case that actions taken in the short term have most of their effects in the long term. A time frame which is too short will capture only the costs of improving compatibility, and not the benefits.

Intellectual capital: An important variation of the ROI argument concerns management of intellectual capital (Stewart, 1989). Maximization of intellectual capital is the mission of education and training enterprises, and valuation of intellectual capital could be used as the basis of meaningful cost-benefit analysis for these organizations. The impact on intellectual capital by various technology investments within the enterprise thus could be measured, and a meaningful cost-benefit analysis performed. This approach provides a way to provide meaningful cost-benefit analyses for technologies which resist more traditional means of analysis. For example, in many education and training organizations, there is no obvious way to gauge the benefits of the Internet. However, an effective intellectual capital management strategy is likely to make extensive use of the Internet as a means for knowledge capture and dissemination, all with much less time delay, greater access, and with lower cost than with traditional methods for these functions, such as creation of paper-based libraries. By valuing the assets thus created, a meaningful cost-benefit picture for the investment in Internet technology is feasible for the first time.

Effects on Organizational Capability

Many applications of technology in education and training involve instruction delivered by use of technology, but many do not. Applications of both kinds have the potential of improving the organization's ability to achieve its mission. For example, Technology can be used to improve the timeliness, completeness and usability of data for the purpose of decision-making. Using computers it is quite feasible to develop a near-real-time picture of each individual learner's progress, by use of software to automate testing, marking, record keeping and reporting, as well as personalized assignment.

One of the big problems is that the classroom process is unknown except by the participants. This makes it extremely difficult to change the practices of the organization, and to ensure consistency and currency in what is taught. Technology can be used to provide instructors with data bases of instructional resources, tools and plans which are aligned precisely to clearly defined curriculum standards. The overall effect is improved consistency and responsiveness to change by the organization.

True individualization and self-paced, mastery-model[9] learning often is prohibitively difficult to administer in conventional classrooms. Technology can help, by directly providing some instruction, and by performing the frequent assessment and prescription tasks which mastery learning requires, thus relieving the instructor of a number of "low level" tasks and creating time for more high-value tasks.

One of the common findings for self-instructional use of technology is that time on task by learners increases when compared to conventional classroom methods. Furthermore, if the software is well-designed, rate of responding by individual learners goes up, and quality of responding (thoughtfulness of response) may rise. The net effect is that technology can be used to change the rolc of the instructor, from "sage on the stage" to "guide on the side," by freeing time for the teacher to engage in individual and small-group interaction. In this way, the ability of the organization to change its basic instructional model changes.

Technology applications driven by intents such as these are common in business and industry-based e-Learning (Rosenberg, 2001), but are still fairly rare in academic settings at all levels. In evaluating them, attention should focus on the change in organizational capability, such as successful implementation of change objectives.

---

9. Mastery learning is based on two instructional management principles: the learner should not begin study of a given topic until all prerequisites have been mastered, and the learner should go on to the next topic only after fully mastering each one taught.

It should be clear from this overview that the effects of technology can be varied, even within a single application. It is likely, therefore, that a carefully defined evaluation plan should examine a number of effects: basing the evaluation on a single measure (such as test scores or cost) is likely to fail to capture important technology effects, and may miss the primary goal of the technology's application entirely.

Two additional considerations are important in deciding what to evaluate: whether to attempt to isolate the effects of technology, and whether to evaluate the processes of technology use.

Decision-makers and prospective evaluators of technology often assume that they should isolate the effects of technology from other effects of the training or education program under study. In general, however, we recommend against such attempts, and recommend in favour of studying intact programs. The reasons are based on a basic principle of technology, and a methodological issue.

A basic principle of educational technology is that it always is used within a context (framework) which exists outside the technology, and creates the purpose for its use. Often, learners depend on the instructor to create this framework by relating the technology use to a specific task which supports a larger goal. It is thus a gross oversimplification to portray any learning outcome as solely the product of the technology component(s). Learning outcomes are always a result of the interaction of the learning environment and the learner, and the technology is just one part of the learning environment. Effects due solely to the technology are likely to be relatively insignificant, while interaction effects with various environmental and learner factors are likely to be critically important to the success of the learning experience and the technology. Thus, it is critically important to understand *technology in context*. The goal of evaluation should be to understand the results which occur when technology is used in a particular way, in a particular context. Studying the effects of technology in isolation is typically of much less interest to the practitioner, though it may be a valid research objective.

The methodological reason to study intact programs concerns the cost, intrusiveness and complexity of the study required. Typically, studying technology in context can be done using *case study* and *qualitative* research techniques (see next section). These techniques are very labor-intensive, and require detailed observation and description of the inputs, processes and outputs of the whole learning environment as the evaluator finds it in the school or training organization. By contrast, isolating the effects of technology from the interactions with the rest of the learning environment usually requires a control group study, in which the strategy is to compare the users of technology with a similar group of users who did not use technology.

Another common concern is over the desired length of the study. Again, the recommendation is to study an entire program, where possible, whether the program spans a few days, weeks, or months of use. The reason is that it is usually desirable for the study to avoid "novelty effects" having to do with the initial wave of interest and confusion often associated with introduction of a new technology.

In addition to evaluating the effects of technology, it is often important to examine how the technology is used. First, the same technology is likely to be used differently in every environment in which it is employed. To understand the effects of technology, therefore, it is important to understand how it has been used in a particular environment. Second, technology is rarely used in the way the designers intended, especially during the first iteration of the program. A variety of "startup" or "learning curve" issues usually affect the way in which a technology is used at first. Various technology "glitches" often affect availability and reliability. In addition, both instructors and learners need to learn what the technology does, and how best to use it. Thus it is likely that the technology will not be used in the way the designers intended until the second or later iterations of the education or training program, if ever.

In particular, evaluators should consider examining utilization effects in terms of Consistency in delivery, total quality management, Scalability, time of delivery, and instructional management. The overview of the effects of technology and the framework of evaluation goals is intended to help clarify decisions about what to evaluate. Now we can turn to methodological issues concerned with how to evaluate. The next section will provide an overview of evaluation designs, and provide an overview of cost analysis methodology.

Evaluation Designs

We use an evaluation design to plan how to collect and analyze the information needed to answer evaluation questions. The design includes defining the time and location for collecting information, what groups or individuals will be observed, what types of data collection instruments will be used, how the resulting observations will be analyzed and summarized, and how the results will be presented to support decisions and make value judgments about the object being evaluated. A number of general design strategies planning how to collect information have proven to be useful in so many settings that they have become part of the evaluator's standard toolbox. We will discuss three of these general strategies: experimental and quasi-experimental designs, case studies, and cost analysis.

Experimental and Quasi-Experimental Designs

Experimental designs are particularly useful in evaluating the educational benefits caused by instructional programs by helping us be sure that observed learning gains are a result of the educational program being evaluated and are not caused by other factors. Experimental designs are powerful strategies for establishing the causal relationships between educational programs and learning outcomes. There are many excellent references on the subject (Campbell and Stanley, 1963; Hicks, 1973; Cook, 1991; Netter et. al., 1996.) Three of the most widely used experimental designs are posttest only, pretest and posttest, and factorial designs. Quasi experimental designs are also useful in technology evaluation. A common perception is that experimental designs are "more rigorous" than quasi-experimental designs. In fact, there are trade offs—there are both advantages and disadvantages in using both types of designs of evaluation.

One of the challenging issues in implementing experimental or quasi-experimental designs when evaluating technology programs is being sure that the technology program being studied was actually implemented as intended. Inconsistent or partial implementation can invalidate the most carefully designed study. This is particularly true for technology programs since they are often dispersed across locations. Learners interacting one-on-one with a program may not follow directions or be motivated to attend to the instruction. In addition, technology has a tendency to malfunction or to not perform as expected. Network problems, out of date equipment or operating systems, lack of proper teacher and learner training to use the system, lack of necessary support to maintain the system can all produce ineffective implementation of a program.

On the plus side, computer systems can be used to collect very precise and voluminous data about student use of learning systems. It is possible to track the paths learners take through lessons, the correct or incorrect responses they choose when asked, the amount of time they spend in instruction, and so forth. When judiciously designed, the computer can provide very useful information about learner behaviours and performance. On the other hand, if the data is just being collected because "some day we will figure out what to do with it," experience has shown that the data are often not analyzed and nothing is done with it. Computer records can be so idiosyncratic and complex that no analysis strategy can adequately summarize them.

Case Study Designs

Case study evaluations seek to describe in detail an educational program by developing rich descriptions of one or a few instances of their use in use (Denzin and Lincoln, 2000; Marshall and Rossman, 1999; Yin, 1994). The explanatory power of case studies is the consistency and interconnectedness of observations and other evidence about events. Case methods include observation by researchers or trained participants in a naturalistic setting, interviews with participants, analysis of records, surveys, tests and performance measures, especially if they are part of the regular routine. The goal is depth of information and checking for interconnections and consistency across evidence. Case evaluations are concerned with program elements that are common across sites as well as those characteristics that are unique to the particular site being studied (Shaw, 1999; Stake, 1995).

Case evaluations can provide a richer understanding of the operation and social context of educational programs than can other research designs. Case research helps answer questions like, what parts of the educational program are most effective. Why did a program work (not work) as intended? What else might be included in the program to make it more useful?

Another benefit of case study methods is they are less obtrusive than experimental procedures. When educators and learners know they are involved in an "experiment" they may act differently than they would in a more typical setting. On the other hand, a weakness of case methods is that one case evaluation does not lend itself to generalizing to other implementations of the program. It takes a collection of cases to begin to see the common elements across cases. In the final analysis it usually takes more time and it may be more expensive to conduct all of the case studies that are needed to confidently identify causal patterns in an educational program. In addition, case methods are not likely to detect effects that are evident only by examining multiple sites within one study or effects that are moderate in size.

Also, because the case evaluator is such a critical part of the instrumentation and analysis of the case, it is often difficult to find evaluators with the proper training and experience to conduct insightful case studies.

When to use case studies? Case studies should be done when there is a premium in the minds of clients on understanding how a technology program works within the context of the entire training setting. This rich understanding can be particularly helpful at the earlier stages of evaluating a program. It is an effective strategy for generating issues to evaluate in broader studies. Case methods are not well suited to establishing causal relationship between program use and learner outcomes, particularly when only one or a few cases are conducted. They are not effective in describing effects that reach outside the limits of the case site. Case methods are not very sensitive in measuring or quantifying effects that are moderate in size or effects that occur over time periods longer than the time covered by the case.

As with other research methods, there is a danger in over interpreting the findings and conclusions from case evaluations. The reports are constructed to tell a story of program implementation and effects. In telling that story case researchers can begin to see patterns that are only partially suggested by the data, or to make generalizations from specific instances that may not be repeated in other settings.

The case study gives us a method for understanding the meaning of technology innovations in terms that matter to the educators and administrators implementing them. When we take a close look at educational institutions, we learn that no proposed technology is value-free to the educators involved. The technology practices proposed will either support the culture and values of the schools or they will seek to change these values. Most technologies arrive on the scene with great fanfare and promise; most are rejected because they are incompatible with the values and organizational goals of schools and the people that work in them (Cuban, 1986; Fullan, 1991; Hodas, 1995; Honey and Moller, 1990; Sarason, 1990). This does not mean that all technology innovations are limited by the existing cultures of schools. Case methods help define the contextual social issues that must be addressed in technology innovations.

The Internet can be used for Case Studies of Technology. Mann and Stewart (2000) have developed a handbook for conducting online qualitative research. An excellent chapter is devoted to ethical issues for conducting online research, including fair information processing, informed consent, and confidentiality.

Return on Investment

The underlying ideas of cost analysis are easy to understand. The analysis procedures are an extension of familiar budgeting and instructional design activities. (see Kearsley, 1982; Levin, 1983; or Swanson and Gradous, 1988.) Furthermore, it is not always necessary to do long and expensive studies to get useful information. With "quick and dirty" cost projections we can often obtain useful estimates of a program's financial value. There are several methodologies for estimating RoI. These are Basic Input-Outcome Model with four variations which are commonly used in evaluation and decision making: cost-benefit analysis, cost-effectiveness analysis, cost-utility analysis, and cost-feasibility analysis (Levin, 1983).

As mentioned earlier, a common application of cost-efficiency studies in educational technology concerns uses of technology to improve access. The goal is to provide services which are of comparable quality to conventional classroom instruction, but without the costs of creating such environments for these students. Central to cost-benefit analysis is successful measurement of benefits. Cost-benefit analysis (and sometimes cost-utility analyses) requires dollar estimates of program outcomes. These estimates must be reasonably accurate and credible to be useful. We may only be able to generate credible dollar estimates for some of the outcomes of a program. Nevertheless, even partial estimates of benefits can be useful.

A general approach can be used for estimating the dollar value of program outcomes (Tracey, 1985; Swanson and Gradous, 1988). This approach can be summarized into three steps. First, define the outcome desired in terms of a concrete performance or desired condition. Second, set baseline and target levels for the performance. Third, calculate the dollar value of increasing performance from baseline to target levels. Yet, in principle, there are many worthwhile program effects that we cannot value in dollars.

Four steps are involved in combining outcomes into a single rating (see Levin, 1983):

1. Have stakeholders rank the importance of achieving the mastery levels set for each outcome. Statements can be rated on a scale of 10 to 0, with 10 being great importance and 0 being no importance.
2. On each outcome, determine the percentage achievement for each program being compared. Baseline performance is 0 per cent and the mastery level is 100 per cent. A program that scored halfway between the baseline and mastery level would be transformed to 50 per cent.
3. For each program, multiply the percentage of outcome mastery scores by the importance rating for the outcome.
4. Sum the resulting products to obtain a composite score for each program. The program with the highest rating is the one of most worth.

Note, what we would be doing here is hybrid cost-effectiveness and cost-utility analysis if the original outcome data came from actual performance but the combining of outcomes measures were done by rater judgments.

As with any other evaluation study, cost analysis findings cannot be used mechanically to make decisions. We should view these studies as a source of information rather than a source of decisions. All evaluations, including cost analysis studies, are imperfect because input and outcome values used in the studies are estimates suffering from imprecision in measurement and uncertainty of the future. Furthermore, cost analysis does not consider all important variables to consider in making decisions. For example, contextual and process variables are not included in a cost analysis.

Obviously, we should not treat all differences as meaningful. When possible, we should use appropriate statistical tests to determine if apparent differences in outcomes or costs are plausibly random differences between groups.

However, even if "statistically significant" differences exist, we should screen findings for practical significance. Levin (1983) has suggested that the differences of less than 10 per cent to 20 per cent between input-outcome ratios should be ignored; other information should be considered for deciding between programs. Differences between ratios of greater than 100 per cent ought to be taken seriously. However, choosing between programs must still consider all information about the programs.

Measurement Strategies

The measurement strategies fall into one of four categories: self-report instruments, observation procedures, utilization records, and learning outcomes. A typical evaluation study uses several if not all of these types of measures in a coordinated way. By "triangulating" data from different instruments and procedures it is possible to get a better picture of the situation than by relying too much on any one measure.

Self Report Instruments

Self-report instruments allow participants to tell us about the program being evaluated, including how they used the program, what they felt about the experience, where they think the program can be improved, and their overall judgment of the program's worth. These instruments also allow respondents to describe themselves and background or contextual information. Self-reports can be obtained through interviews, questionnaires, and through attitude scales.

Of course, when we are asking for self-reports in interviews, surveys, or in attitude scales we are assuming that the respondent understands our questions more or less as we do. We are assuming that they know the information we are asking about and they are willing to give us complete and truthful answers. The validity of these assumptions needs to be examined whenever we plan to use self-report procedures.

An interview is a purposeful discussion with a participant

about the program and issues surrounding it. We not only hear their answers but can ask follow-up questions to clarify responses or to pursue unanticipated issues. This flexibility of interviews makes them a valuable technique, particularly in the early stages of an evaluation when we are discovering and refining the key issues to study.

Depending upon the circumstances, a good interviewer may be able to schedule and conduct from one to eight interviews per day, depending upon how easy it is to contact respondents, how flexible their schedule is, how cooperative they are, and how long the interview lasts. Interviews can be conducted face-to-face, by phone, or, for more technologically adept respondents, by Internet email or live chat.

Interviews differ in how structured they are in asking questions and pursuing side issues. In an unstructured interview, an experienced interviewer needs only a general agenda of issues to cover; the interviewer is free to pursue new issues as they naturally come up in the conversation. The interviewer is also free to add or subtract issues from the agenda as the interview progresses. When done by a skilled interviewer, an unstructured interview provides the respondent the best chance to "tell their story" and to structure the issues the way they see it. They are more likely to bring up issues not anticipated by the evaluator, and therefore provide original insights into how the participants perceive the program being evaluated.

Questionnaires

Questionnaires can be handed out to respondents in groups, can be mailed to respondents, and can be distributed through the Internet by email or web sites. In any format questionnaires can include both free-response and fixed-choice questions. Free-response questions allow the respondent to write answers in their own words. A fixed-choice questions provide the respondent with predetermined options to choose among. Most surveys include a combination of free-response items and fixed-choice items.

Four types of fixed-choice items are widely used in surveys:

- A checklist is a series of choices that are responded to by checking all that meet a specified criteria.
- an inventory allows respondents to list the names of things or enumerate the items or events that meet a certain condition.
- Rankings and ratings both involve making quantitative judgments about some group of objects, persons, activities, or ideas. Rankings are for choosing between options but will not reveal if the respondent believes any of the items are good or bad as a set. Ratings on the other hand involves comparing things to a scale.

Attitude Scales

Often in an evaluation it is important to measure respondents' attitudes toward some aspect of the program. In these instances the evaluator includes several rating items within the questionnaire with the intent of summing the ratings for these items into one score. Attitude scales are interpreted by comparing individuals or groups to one another.

Observation

As with interviews, observation can be unstructured or structured. The general procedure for unstructured observations are as follows (Guba and Lincoln, 1981):

1. Prepare for observation by having preliminary discussions with people from the site and by studying available reports and descriptive information.
2. Develop some initial questions and hypotheses about what should be focused on in the evaluation observations.
3. Looking *at* (not for) what happens. Listening to what is said to you and others.
4. Ask questions to clarify what you are seeing and hearing.
5. Assimilate and synthesize information—regular off-site thinking time.

6. Check observations against initial questions and hypotheses, changing questions and hypotheses to fit observations.
7. Through repeated observations triangulate findings, cross-check conclusions, look for confirming and disconfirming information.

Structured observations, like structured interviews, utilize formal written questions, checklists, and data collection forms to guide the observer. There are collections of forms that may be used or modified for evaluating educational programs (Simon and Boyer, 1974). As with interviews, it is important that observers be trained to properly use the observation protocol so that valid and reliable data is obtained.

Utilization of Records

Computer instruction programs often generate a wealth of information about learner use of the system. The data collected by computer systems often fall into one of three categories: time data, artifacts or entries, and sequence of options and paths taken. Time data shows the schedule and length of study sessions on the computer. Time on task may be an important instructional variable that may or may not, depending on the students and the instructional strategy used correlate with outcome measures. As the learner uses the system they may generate artifacts, such as writing samples, graphic presentations, or other reports, that can be used in evaluating the program.

Finally, for courses that allow users to control the sequence and topic of learning experiences, the paths that learners take while going through can also be very useful. Following the paths taken may show the differences between high scoring and lower scoring learners. Students who do not appear to be following a clear strategy of going through the courses may need additional guidance in the course. Students who skip instructional modules to only take the testing sections may be trying to "game" the program and avoid spending the time learning the content needed. Looking at the paths taken can give insight into these patterns.

Learning Outcome Measures

Tests: The literature on testing is extensive; we will only touch upon a few issues regarding achievement testing here. Achievement tests measure a learner's understanding of specific content by having the learner engage in some mental behaviour regarding that content. The tests used in evaluating program outcomes should be valid for this purpose. This means the test should cover the objectives set for the program and test the content at the cognitive level intended for the program.

Achievement test items are usually scored as being right or wrong with the number of right answers being summed for a total test score. The test scores can be compared against the sub-areas of the content covered or the behaviours assessed.

Performance-based measures: Performance-based measures are developed with the same motive as other achievement tests: to assess learned knowledge and cognitive ability. The difference is that performance-based measures examine learner performance in real-life situations: while the learner is engaged in performing some authentic task. Performance tests may involve an arranged (simulated) situation, e.g. writing a formatted letter on a word processor.

Performance measures usually are considered to be more valid than written tests because of greater contextual and response authenticity. The behaviour tested is observed in a context more like the target outcome desired and the learner displays behaviour that is more like the final behaviour wanted. However, performance tests cannot usually cover the breadth of content covered in a written test nor can they provide the number of testing activities included in a typical written test.

Conclusion

There is greater need, and greater demand, for evaluation of technology than at any time in the past generation. However, although thousands of studies have been published over the 40-year life of computer-based learning, only a few hundred are sound enough to be interpretable and useful. Furthermore, far too many expensive programs have yielded little in the way of results. If the promise of computers is to be realized in the everyday practice of education and training, practitioners must invest more effort in evaluation of their programs, and must be more willing to study their programs, than has often been the case historically. The studies we need must be more sophisticated than is usually the case now, and more sophisticated than policy makers often know to request. As professionals, we must steer the policy agenda for research and evaluation of technology away from simplistic studies which are too flawed to tell us anything useful, and toward studies which show a sophisticated awareness of the history of technology evaluation and research, the methodological tradeoffs involved, and the real issues which determine the effectiveness and scalability of technology. Only if we do so will the potential of technology to restructure education and training be realized.

REFERENCES

Campbell, D.T, and Stanley, J.C. *Experimental and quasi-experimental designs for research.* Chicago: Rand McNally, 1963.

Clark, R.E. Evaluating Distance Education: Strategies and Cautions. *The Quarterly Review of Education*, 2000. pp. 3-16.

Cook, T. Quasi-experimental designs. In McLaughlin and Phillips (Eds.) *Evaluation and Education: At Quarter Century.* Chicago: NSSE University of Chicago, 1991.

Cuban, L. *Teachers and machines: The classroom use of technology since 1920.* New York: Teachers College Press, 1986.

Denzin, N.K. and Lincoln, Y.S. *Handbook of qualitative research.* (2nd ed.) Thousand Oaks: Sage Publications, 2000.

Fullan, M.G. *The new meaning of educational change.* New York: Teachers College Press, 1991.

Gagne, R.M., Briggs, L.J., Wager, W.W. *Principles of instructional design (3rd Ed.).* New York: Holt, Rinehart and Winston, 1988.

Glass, G.V., Willson, V.L., and Gottman, J.M. *Design and Analysis of Time-Series Experiments.* Boulder: Associated University Press, 1975.

Heinecke, W.F., Blasi, L., Milman, N., and Washington, L. New Directions in the Evaluation of the Effectiveness of Educational Technology. Presented to The Secretary's Conference on Educational

Technology—1999. ERIC Document # ED 452 025. Downloaded 1/29/02 from http://www.ed/gov/Technology/TechConf/1999. 1999.

Hicks, C.R. *Fundamental concepts in the design of experiments (2nd ed.).* New York: Holt, Rinehart and Winston, 1973.

Hodas, S. *Technology refusal and the organizational culture of schools. http://homepage.seas.upenn.edu/~cpage/techref.html.* February 1, 1995.

Honey, M., & Moeller, B. *Teacher's beliefs and technology integration: Different values, different understandings (Technical Report No. 6).* Center for Technology in Education, 1990.

Honey, M., Culp, K.M., Carrigg, F. Perspectives on Technology and Education Research: Lessons from the Past and the Present. Presented to The Secretary's Conference on Educational Technology—1999. Downloaded 1/29/02 from ttp://www.ed/gov/Technology/TechConf/1999. 1999.

Kearsley, G. *Costs, Benefits, and Productivity in Training Systems.* Reading, MA: Addison-Wesley, 1982.

Levin, H.M. *Cost-effectiveness: A Primer.* Beverly Hills, CA: Sage, 1983.

Lloyd, T. Winning the Budget Battle. *Training,* pp. 57-62, May, 1989.

Lockes, B.B., Burton, J.K., Cross, L.H. No Comparison: Distance Education Finds a New Use for "No Significant Difference." *Proceedings of Selected Research and Development Papers Presented at the National Convention of the Association for Educational Communications and Technology (AECT), Houston, TX, February 10-14, 1999).* ERIC Document # ED 436 176, 1999.

Mann, C. and Stewart, F. *Internet communication and qualitative research: A handbook for researching online.* Thousand Oaks: Sage Publications, 2000.

Marshall, C. and Rossman, G.B. *Designing qualitative research.* (3rd ed.) Thousand Oaks: Sage Publications, 1999.

Maxwell, J.A. *Qualitative research design: An interactive approach.* Thousand Oaks: Sage Publications, 1996.

McCombs, B. Assessing the Role of Educational Technology in the Teaching and Learning Process: A Learner-Centered Perspective. Presented to The Secretary's Conference on Educational Technology—2000. Downloaded 1/29/02 from *http://www.ed/gov/Technology/TechConf/2000*, 2000

Netter, J., Kutner, M.H., Nachtsheim, C.J., and Wasserman, W. *Applied linear statistical models (4th ed.).* Boston: WCB McGraw-Hill, 1996.

Russell, B.H. Social research methods: Qualitative and quantitative approaches. Thousand Oaks: Sage Publications, 1999.

Sarason, S.B. *The predictable failure of educational reform.* San Francisco: Jose-Bass, 1990.

Scriven, M. Modus operandi method. In J.R. Popham (Ed.) *Evaluation in education*. McCutcheon, 1976.

Scriven, M. *Evaluation thesaurus (4th ed.)*. Newbury Park, CA: Sage, 1991.

Shaw, I. *Qualitative evaluation*. Thousand Oaks: Sage Publications, 1999.

Spencer, L.M. Calculating Costs and Benefits. In W.R. Tracey (Ed.). *Human Resources Management and Development Handbook*. New York: American Management Association, *1985, pp. 1486-151O.*

Spencer, L.M. Calculating Costs and Benefits. In W.R. Tracey (Ed.). *Human Resources Management and Development Handbook*. New York: American Management Association, *1985, pp. 1486-151O.*

Stake, R.E. *The art of case study research*. Thousand Oaks: Sage Publications, 1995.

Swanson, R.A., and Gradous, D.B. *Forecasting Financial Benefits of Human Resource Development*. San Francisco: Jossey Bass, 1988.

Tashakkori, A. and Teddlie, C. *Mixed methodology: Combining qualitative and quantitative approaches*. Thousand Oaks: Sage Publications, 1998.

Worthen, B.R., and Sanders, J.R. *Educational evaluation: Alternative approaches and practical guidelines*. White Plains, NY: Longman, 1987.

Yin, R.K. *Case study research: Design and methods*. Newbury Park: Sage Publications, 1994.

9

Beyond Educational Technology

MARMAR MUKHOPADHYAY

Teaching-learning, the central core of educational technology is the subset of education. Hence, the relevance and role of teaching and learning has to be seen in the context of education—its nature, goals and purposes. To that extent, teaching and learning and educational technology is only as good as it serves the purposes of education. The knowledge development in the field of teaching-learning and educational technology has put us at crossroads. On one hand, there have been tremendous developments in teaching-learning methodologies and educational technology; on the other, the philosophical discourses on education, over the ages, continues to explore its nature and purpose vis-à-vis the human nature and its potentialities. Such philosophical discourse is an endless journey across time; it is not a target. Contemporary research and experiments are also branching off to examine relevance and transferability of training techniques applied to other animals (*homo-sapiens*) to the domains of human development; Blanchard (2002) derived implications from training of killer whales.

Educational technology—both as a concept and practice—has also evolved over a period; accordingly, new tools and techniques have been added to its repertoire. It has traversed the path of innovation, creativity and exploration. The major issue at hand is whether and how far such developments in the teaching-learning methodologies and educational technology contribute to the very process of education, its

---

Joint Director, NIEPA, New Delhi, India

purposes, goals and cherished values. In this chapter, I propose to revisit education, corroborate with the developments in teaching-learning and educational technology in that context, and look beyond.

Revisiting Education

Conventionally, education has been equated with schooling at all levels of formal education. Emphasis has been on learning of subjects, mastering specific branches of structured knowledge systems. Exceptions apart, emphasis is narrow, on the learning of schools subjects. In the enthusiasm and excitement of teaching 'Latin', poor 'John' has been forgotten (remember Sir John Adams' classic statement describing teaching, 'Teacher Teaches John, Latin'). The cognitive development as indicated by higher-order cognition, different levels of thinking (skills) are not only beyond the scope of articulated goals of schooling, there is no deliberate design and effort in teaching thinking and other basic skills of learning to learn. Thus, education as equated with schooling, has a narrow end and focus. In this section, we will explore the concept of education, its nature and purpose from a few different stands.

Life provides us a larger colourful canvas painted with wide range of positive and negative emotions, physical beauty coupled with pains and pleasures, intricate skills, multiplicity of intelligences and cognitive processes and a variety of levels of spirituality. Thus, education as schooling of our times seems far too small and narrow for life. To corroborate this larger view, education has been defined as 'preparation for life'. I have serious doubt about the concept of education as preparation for life, if it means only the economic life. This narrow-band concept is derived from the economic platform where education is seen as means of human capital formation. This is not only undermining the human genius, but also equating a subset (income generating skills) with the set (human being). Life moves through several phases like infancy, childhood, adolescence, youth, middle age and old age. In Indian tradition, life has been seen in four phases: *Brahmacharya* (Period of celibacy and learning), *Garhasthya* (Household life), *Banaprastha* (detachment within family life) and *Nirvana* (life of renunciation). Schooling, from pre-school till university degree spans over 20 years. It is part of life, hence life itself. The first twenty to 25 years of studentship and *Brahmacharya* is the most creative phase of life; dedicating such prime-time to prepare for the non-creative phase of adulthood or Garhasthya and age of Banaprastha and Nirvana is an unwise investment. Schooling must be seen as life itself. To that extent, education (as schooling) is nurturing the seeds of potentialities hidden in every human being.

Life is concerned with living. According to Vedantic wisdom, human beings live in four planes, namely physical, mental, intellectual and spiritual. This four-plane living paradigm has been professed in the Report of the International Commission for Education in 21st Century to UNESCO, Learning: The Treasure Within, more popularly known as Delor's Commission (UNESCO, 1996). Important spirit is the linkage between learning and the treasure within; learning as the means of unearthing, nurturing and enriching the treasure within. This easily derives inspiration from Swami Vivekananda's definition of education as 'manifestation of perfection already in man' (woman). Thus, business of education is optimizing the physical, mental, intellectual, and spiritual potentials of life; optimizing not in unrelated streams, but also integrating them together so that life represents the totality. Issue is what is that potentiality in human beings?

Human Beings: Interfaith Knowledge

Prophet Mohammed described human beings as made in the image of God. According to Christian philosophy, human beings are Viceroy of God on earth. According to Hindu wisdom, human beings are children of God; similar sentiments are echoed in Baha'i philosophy (Mukhopadhyay, 2003). Mystic poet Kahlil Gibran contended that children are through the parents but from God (Gibran, 1997). There is a significant convergence, rather concurrence, about the nature of human beings across religious traditions that were born and nurtured in different soils. Firstly, he/she has been defined only with reference to divinity. Hence, by implication, the potentiality of the human being is self-realization or achieving divine qualities. Human beings are capable of reaching divinity and that total consciousness. Lord Jesus, Prophet Mohammed, Martin Luther King, Mother Teresa, innumerable saints of Hindu tradition represent that ultimate development in human body and consciousness. Thus charter of education is optimization of the physical, mental, intellectual and spiritual potentialities.

Four Planes of Living

From the ancient 'Charak Samhita' that is the foundation stone of the Indian Ayurvedic tradition to the modern-day, brain research findings are consistent that only part of the physical potential has so far been explored and exploited. That only 10 to 15 per cent brain cells have so far been activated (Rastak, 2002), indicates one such phenomena. Leonard Orr (1998), in his book *Breaking the Death Habits* contended that humans are born immortal but they develop the habit of dying. Thus, there is a long way to go before the total physical potential is unfolded. Orr claims to have met persons living for 300 years in the same body, 'mostly in Indian Himalayas'.

There is a vast body of knowledge on the intellectual development of the human beings. Also, such knowledge has resulted into massive diversity of views on the nature of intelligence. On one hand, starting with Spearman's concept of general intelligence and specific intelligence, intelligence has been defined as abstract, concrete, social and other forms. Howard Gardener's multiple intelligence theory revolutionizes the concept of intelligence and challenges various established contentions. It is also established that beyond the teens, intelligence do not grow. However, certain other dimensions of intelligence grow, e.g. emotional intelligence (Goleman, 1995) till the end. Human knowledge has thus covered large grounds in understanding the nature of intelligence and its role in life.

Human emotions have been a major area of study. The

hierarchy of educational objectives of the affective domain by Benjamin Bloom (1956) is one of the early efforts in integrating education to emotional aspect of life. On the nature and development of emotions and emotional intelligence, massive new light has been shed (Goleman, 1995). As mentioned earlier, Goleman claims that emotional intelligence can be developed and learnt till the last moment of life. More significant impact of research on emotional intelligence is the growing evidence that human performance is, significantly, the function of emotional intelligence than 'cognitive intelligence' which was given the supremacy so far. More rational statement would be that in terms of human performance academic or cognitive intelligence is the necessary condition; emotional intelligence forms the sufficient condition. Almost without exception, the books on self-development substantively covers the issues of learning to manage the emotional aspect of life (e.g. Your Erroneous Zones, You can win, Born to win, Ageless Body, Timeless Mind, Tough time Never last, But Tough People Do, etc.). Explorations on the vast potential of emotional life as determinant of quality of life are yet only the tip of the iceberg.

As interfaith knowledge defines human being as a spiritual-self or spiritual configuration, its potentiality is traversing the distance from beastliness to divinity; the divine potential is indicated by love and compassion, the very core of Christian, Hindu, Islam, Baha'i, Sikh, Buddhist, and all other religious traditions. However, large majority of human beings are still trapped into hatred, distrust and other such demonic attributes. 20th century witnessed the wanton killings and massive destruction of the weaker nations and communities at the hands of informed and empowered nations. The beginning of 21st century has been far worse. Thus, the spiritual potential has remained almost untapped for majority of the people in the world. Education, schooling, has not contributed to the development of this aspect of human life.

There is another more mundane but important view about spirituality. The word, 'Spirituality', is derived from 'spirit'. Spirit or urge for exploring the unknown. Desmond Hillary and Tenzing Norgay, otherwise a Christian and a Buddhist, scaled the Himalayan peek because of the urge to conquer. Urge to conquer nature and space, adventures into new thoughts and creativity, innovations are, from this angle, the spiritual quality of mind. Different educational systems indicate how this creative urge or spirituality are either cultivated or killed. Largely, in large parts of the world, schooling does not foster spirit of adventure and creativity; on the contrary, it fosters with tremendous force, convergent thinking and concurrence to tradition.

Learning: The Treasure Within

The second complementary paradigm of education presented by the Delor's Commission reflects the matured human wisdom. Among many concepts, the four pillars of learning, namely 'learning to know', 'learning to do', 'learning to live together' and 'learning to be' caught the imagination of scholars all over the world. In learning to know, the report brings in the concept of 'learning to learn' along with mastery of the knowledge systems. Learning to do implies the ability to convert learning into action. Learning to live together unveils the critical social dimension for the survival of the civilization. With the developments in the nuclear science and technology particularly warheads strewn in various parts of the world, the human destruction is seconds away. The only defence against such social and civilizational catastrophe is learning to live together. This cannot be achieved by building tolerance; the foundation is respect for other religions and cultures, social mores and practices (UN Meeting of Religious Leaders). 'Learning to be' points out to the spiritual self, hidden in the human beings. 'To be' is different from 'to become'. Contemporary conventional education nurtures the ambition to become (a teacher, a doctor, etc.) defined largely by profession or vocation. 'To be' is all inclusive and at a higher pedestal. Important concept presented by the Commission is in the title, *Learning: The Treasure Within*. Learning is to explore and optimize the treasure (potential within) that can be built up on the four pillars of learning. The philosophic underpinning of Delor's Report coincides with and echoes Vedantic wisdom.

Educatedness

The word 'educated' has been associated conventionally with qualified people; people who have been tested by an authorized agency like a school board or a university and certified to have passed their qualifying examination. What a qualified person represent is minimum level of mastery of certain subjects. It is not unusual to experience differentiation between a 'qualified person' and a 'liberated person' or a 'cultured person' and the like implying that neither all qualified persons possess a cultured mind or are liberated from narrow walls of recognition by caste, religion, language, etc. nor all liberated and cultured persons are qualified from school or college. Or, even if there are qualified and liberated people, the liberation is indeed due to schooling.

This raises a serious doubt about the nature of educatedness. Keeping the nature of human beings as derived from interfaith knowledge, I have argued elsewhere, educatedness is a multi-component phenomenon organized in a taxonomic structure (Mukhopadhyay, 1999). Being informed is the lowest level of the educatedness hierarchy. The illiterate farmers, housewives, day labourers as well as the school and university graduates are informed though all are not qualified. The difference is in the nature of the information processing. A graduate possesses certified information on a particular discipline as a part of a known knowledge system or discipline; an illiterate farmer carries the functional knowledge of farming drawing from Physics, Chemistry, Botany, Biotechnology and host of other subjects. The farmer lacks the formal qualification and the structure of known knowledge systems. Both are, however, informed; the qualified ones are certified knowledge owners.

The second level in the hierarchy of educatedness is 'being cultured'—what emanates from a human being (warmth, love, appreciation, concern for others, etc.) is culture. The way one treats oneself, others, plants and animals, environment, private and public space, objects, etc. are the indications of culturedness. Vinoba Bhave illustrated this beautifully when he described human reaction to food in three different conditions—'eating when hungry is nature, eating when not hungry is perversion and giving away the food to another hungry person depriving one's own hunger is culture (*sanskriti*).

The third level of the hierarchy is the emancipatedness. Purpose of education is liberating (*sa vidya ya vimuktaye*); liberating from narrow geographical, linguistic, religious, caste and similar other identities, without losing one's roots. A practicing Hindu or a Muslim or a Christian can appreciate and respect other religious traditions and practices.

The final stage of the hierarchy is self-actualization. Unlike the limited view of self-actualization as optimization of one's intellectual potential, the self-actualization implies actualization of full potentiality of the human beings in physical, mental, intellectual and spiritual planes. These four stages of the educateness is not spread over to different periods of life; rather every phase has all the four components of being informed, cultured, emancipated and self-actualized. The business of education is to trigger off those processes by which the human being can actualize all his/her potential in every stage of life.

These three different paradigms of four living planes, four pillars of learning and educatedness are interlinked concepts and frameworks. Together they offer an interesting 3-D model of education.

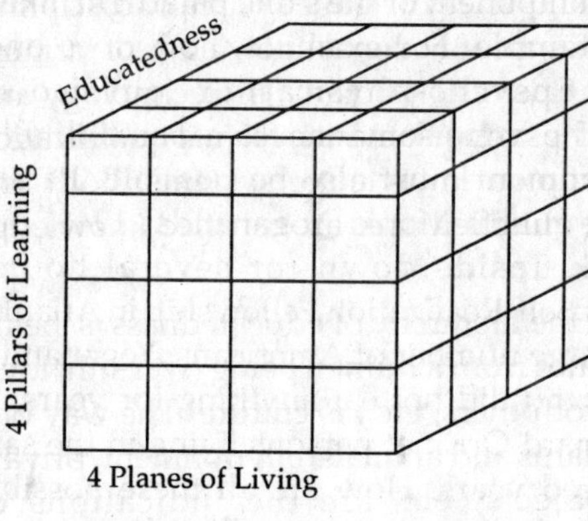

Fig. 1: 3-D Model of Education

The 3-D model represents a rubric cube of 64 components. Out of the 64 cubes one cube contains the 3-dimensions of intellectual plane (out of 4 planes of living), learning to know (out of 4 Pillars of Learning) and informed (out of 4 levels of educatedness) exercised in schooling. Thus, schooling is concerned with just about one of the 64 cubes; 63 other combinations remaining largely unattended, or only marginally attended. Education is challenged to cover the entire spectrum and all components of the rubric cube. To that extent the challenge is *development beyond academics.*

As an alternative illustration, the nature of the challenge can be understood if we combine in another cube, the 3-dimensions as physical plane, learning to live together, and emancipatedness. What kind of education can be conceptualized to contribute for optimization of physical potential, learning to live together with emancipation. Another example is the cube with its 3-dimensions as the spiritual plane, learning to be and self-actualization where all the 3-dimensions are complementary. The anatomical details of the rubric cube presents different sets of challenges where all three dimensions are supplementary and complementary to one another. Considering that the inherent unity of purpose of education is development of human life to its full potential, it requires serious designing and creativity to fulfill the goals of education.

It is also possible to see the role of education by combining more than one component of the same paradigm, like 4 planes of living, for example. For example, how does one design education for psycho-physical or physico-spiritual development. If psycho-somatism is a possibility, physico-spiritual development must also be possible. Paramahansa Yogananda, the Hindu Monk (Yogananda, 1946) buried his head and neck upside down for several hours in the Headquarters of Self-Realization Fellowship in Atlanta in USA in full view of large number of Americans. Yoganandaji wrote about Giribala who did not eat anything for years, yet alive and active. Leonard Orr met persons living in the same body for three hundred years. How are all these possible? Such human excellence indicate dramatically different possibilities.

It is not a utopia. We need not lose such an important possibility either due to our arrogance of knowledge or sheer innocence, though no established science answers such questions. How did they develop such skills? What was their education like? The Knowledge assessment of education from this perspective would indicate that we are still probably 'collecting pebbles on the sea-shore'.

Educational Technology: Thus Far

As mentioned earlier, teaching and learning and educational technology is only as good as it supports the nature and goals of education. The educational technology has been concerned with optimizing human learning and also with economics of learning, learning at the highest level and at least time and cost. Although educational technology has conventionally restricted itself to optimization of cognitive learning and processes, this limitation is artificial since it has acted at the behest of the contention that education is schooling.

The subjects of educational technology include instructional design and systems theory, programmed teaching and classroom transactions, individualized learning, self-learning methodologies, interactive learning, learning assessment, etc. Several methods have been developed on individualized learning, self instructional learning, group-paced learning, interactive learning, situated learning, etc. The whole range of methodologies like programmed instruction, personalized system of instruction, instruction based on self instructional material, audio and video aided instruction, computer aided instruction, web based instruction, online education, video conferencing, audio conferencing, computer conferencing, etc. are the variety of methodologies that contribute to different approaches to instruction and learning.

In the 1960s, there was a massive spurt in research in classroom transactions spearheaded by Ned A. Flanders. Although Flanders Interaction Analysis Category System (FIACS) aimed at assessing the ratio between direct and indirect transactions, it landed up in finding that the FIACS largely measures the effective or emotional transactions in classrooms. The application of transactional analysis in classroom communication also indicates the interplay of different ego states of the teacher in not only transacting with a student but also in the nature of delivery and transaction of the subjects in the classroom (Mukhopadhyay and Saxena, 1982). There are other interesting experiments and practices in training in expression of feelings—students are expected to respond to the daily attendance calls with a statement of feeling. It will be, however, difficult to construe that schooling has as one of its significant objectives, the development of the emotional life and quality of the learners.

It is possible to develop instructional design for affective development (Reigeluth, 1999), instructional designs have primarily been concerned with transactional methodologies for learning of subjects, or for cognitive development. Instructional designing in sports and physical education is very much a possibility and practice. It is also possible in spiritual education and development. There is a definite design in imparting spiritual education by the spiritual Gurus in different religious traditions. Indeed, in Hinduism, place of Guru is highly exalted; it insists that certain spiritual learning and experience is not possible without Guru. But Guru makes his/her own design differently for different disciples—Differentiated Instructional Design (DID, Mukhopadhyay and Parhar, 2001).

It would be evident that educational technology, in tune with the concept and parameters of schooling has contributed primarily, if not exclusively, to the mastery of subjects and to some extent to cognitive development. The education on all other planes have remained largely beyond its purview.

There are accumulated knowledge and debates about the effectiveness of various such methodologies even within the cognitive domain. Since such debates have been more elaborately dealt with by other contributors in this volume, it may not be of much use visiting those issues in this chapter once again. The *summum bonum* of our knowledge assessment of the available research literature is that various teaching-learning methodologies have not only made major contributions to increase the effectiveness of the teaching learning process, but also provided the platform for differential applications. This also implies that effectiveness of instructional methodologies is not uniform across place and time. There is a social context, a cultural context of an institution, and people—teachers and students who inhabit such institutions.

Research on teaching-learning has also highlighted the issues of cost and cost-effectiveness. There are innumerable studies that compare relative effectiveness of different instructional strategies on student learning and corresponding costs. For example, despite the popular perception, the international review indicate that online education is still a costly alternative without conclusive evidence of its effectiveness (Bates, 2002). This is just one illustration of the on-going debate about the relevance and superiority of different teaching learning methodologies over others that are professed by educational technology. Thus, in some sense, educational technology has not been able to offer a rather universally acceptable and effective instructional methodology.

Adopting a utopian agenda, may be a 'necessary utopia' as contended by the Delor's Commission, that education for 21st Century will have to adopt a holistic view of developing human beings at all levels of the life and living. What does our known knowledge of educational technology has to offer for education in the spiritual plane, learning to live together or learning to do? More importantly, how to link and integrate them together so that all the human potentials in all planes blossom fully. Available knowledge in educational technology does not inspire enough confidence that it can handle all aspects of human development.

Over the years, particularly with the advent of technological gadgets, educational technology has been equated with technology in education rather than a product of 'technology of education' and 'technology in education' (Percival and Ellington, 1984). The basic framework, technology of education, has steadily been lost. As a result, the direct teaching or classroom processes have been undermined in the new framework of educational technology since it does not necessarily involve any form of technology in education. The issue needs revisitation. The role of teacher in human development may have to be reconstructed.

The non-cognitive aspects of human development are deeply ingrained in human psyche like value systems in human life that guides our day to day action. Such attributes are largely inculcated through imitation of role models, especially in early years of life. The new literature in managerial psychology professes 'walking the talk' and pace setting as important means of influencing and leading people. What kind of methodology could actually set in the process of inculcation of these higher human attributes?

At this point, it is worth visiting some unusual quarters of human development, namely Hindu Gurukulas, Islamic Centers for education of Maulavies, Center for education of Christian Brothers and Nuns, Buddhist Monastries, etc. to draw lessons for developing the higher human qualities. Such traditions host great wisdom. Let us take the case of a recent development in educational technology, multi-channel learning systems.

There is a reasonable amount of literature on multichannel learning systems (Anzalone 1995, Mukhopadhyay 1995). The major contention is that human learning can be facilitated by using multiple channels that can supplement one another, yet allow an individual to choose the channel that best fits his/her learning styles. Although the multichannel learning literature surfaced with the International Multichannel Action Group on Education (IMAGE) in the mid 1990s, Indian Gurukula tradition followed multichannel learning systems:

One-quarter of learning accrues from the teacher,
Another from self learning
The third from the peer group learning
And, the fourth only with time (experiential learning).

(Hastana Satak)

In the Gurukulas, the Guru[10] taught students through selective discourses. A significant amount of time was left to students to learn by themselves and seek clarifications from the teacher. This self-study followed by interactive learning is further beautifully clarified in *Bhagavad-Gita*, '*pranipatena pariprashnena sevaya*'—learning can be achieved by asking questions and raising doubts with respect and regards to the teacher. The important component is the rider 'questioning with respect' implying receptivity and genuine inquisitiveness, rather than arrogant effort to embarrass the teacher; differentiating between humility of learning from arrogance of knowledge.

Each Guru used to have number of pupils at home staying together and learning together. The staying and learning together, the ancient form of residential schooling, provided them the opportunity of interacting with one another and in groups; Guru also encouraged them to solve problems in groups. This peer group learning not only helped in achieving higher levels of cognition, but also helped develop number of social and emotional skills. Whenever a student's course was completed, the teacher emphasized on his/her ability to learn throughout life. The emphasis was on learning with time and experience.

Within this well considered multichannel learning systems, there are many subtleties. The learners stayed with the teacher in his family; he/she had to fetch woods, fruits, etc. from the forest for both themselves as well as for the Guru's family. The wife of the Guru, called the Gurumaa (mother), cooked and fed all the learners as she fed her own children. The learners learnt to live together, and actively shared the family life. It was part of their life. Since the learners stayed with the Guru's family, Guru's entire life was completely exposed. Unlike today, there was no distinction between the private and public life of the Guru.

---

10. Guru is conceptually different from teacher or *Shikshak*. A teacher or *shikshak* is one who teaches mathematics or geography or another school subject. Guru is the one who 'dispels darkness' by connecting the learner to higher consciousness. Guru is not a subject teacher; he/she takes complete charge of a learner and lifts the soul.

The Guru was not only a learned person but also a practising spiritual being. His typical day would comprise cleaning and taking bath in the early morning followed by meditation and worshipping the God. Only after that, he would teach and give discourses to the students. Gurus own learning habits and his other household activities and day-to-day life were fully visible to the learners. Thus there was no formal value education, but there was value inculcation through role modelling. Guru's life was an open book for learning the living.

Learners followed Guru's life and practised cleaning, meditation and attentive listening to Guru's discourses on higher values of life (learning to be), life skills (learning to do) and living with other learners in Guru's family (learning to live together). Learning of Ashtanga Yoga under the instruction of the Guru provided the physio-spiritual strength to the body that has been described as abode of God in Sikhism. But this did not cost excellence in cognitive development. That learners specialized in different branches of knowledge including medicine, surgery, architecture, etc. indicates the development of cognitive aspects (Das, 1986).

This all round development in the Gurukulas is backed up by sound philosophical underpinnings about nature and purpose of education. The *Taittariya Upanishad* described education as the meeting point of the student and the teacher, discarding the concept of hierarchy between the teacher and the student as possessor and dispenser of knowledge and student as the empty can. Conceptually, both Guru and the disciple are learners.

Conclusion

The old Indian Gurukula system may not be replicable in the newly industrialized model of education. This, however, brings in the importance of human teacher for the holistic development of the learners. Whereas educational technology can assist human learning at its elemental level in cognitive areas, for full human development at higher level of consciousness, it is necessary to look beyond educational technology.

REFERENCES

Anzalone, S., The case for multi-channel learning, in Anzalone, S. (ed).*Multi-channel Learning: Connecting All to Education*, Washington D.C.: EDC, 1995.

Bates, T. *National Strategies on e-Learning*, Paris: IIEP, 2002.

Blanchard, Ken and Others, *Whale Done*, London: Nicholas Bealey, 2002.

Bloom, Benjamin, *Taxonomy of Educational Objectives: The Classification of Educational Goals, Handbook II Affective Domain*, New York: David Mckay, 1956.

Chopra, D., *Ageless Body, Timeless Mind*, London: Riders, 1993.

Das, Santosh K., *The Educational System of the Ancient Indian Hindus*, New Delhi: Gyan, 1986.

Dyer, W.W., *Your erroneous zones*, New York: Harper Collins, 1995. Gardner, Howard, Frame of Mind: *The Theory of Multiple Intelligence*, London: *Basic Books, 1993.*

Gibran, K., *The Prophet*, New Delhi: UBSPD, 1997

Goleman, D. *Emotional Intelligence*, London: Bantam, 1995

Goleman, D. *The New Leaders: Transforming Art of Leadership into Science of Results*, London: Little Brown, 2002.

James, M. and Jongewood, D. *Born to Win*, New York: Penguine, 1971.

Khera, Shiv, *You can win*, New Delhi: McMillan, 1998.

Orr, L. *Breaking the Death Habit: The Science of Everlasting Life*, California: Frog Ltd. 1998.

Mukhopadhyay, Marmar (ed), *Education for a Global Society: Interfaith Dimension*, New Delhi: Shipra, 2003.

Mukhopadhyay, Marmar and Saxena, A.B. Transactional Analysis and Teacher Classroom Behaviour, *RIE* (USA) July, 1982 (also microfiche for International circulation by ERIC, USA).

Mukhopadhyay, Marmar Taxonomy of Educatedness, *University News*, 37(26), June 28, 1999.

Mukhopadhyay, Marmar and Parhar, Madhu, Instructional design in Multi-channel Learning Systems, *British Journal of Educational Technology*, 32(5), November, 2001.

Percival, F. and Ellington, H. *A Handbook of Educational Technology*, London: Kogan Page, 1984.

Reigeluth, C.M. (ed), *Instructional Design Theories and Models: A New paradigm of Instructional Theory*, London: Lawrence Erlbaum, 1999.

UNESCO, *Learning: The Treasure Within*, Paris: UNESCO, 1996.

Yogananda, Paramahansa, *Autobiography of a Yogi*, California: Crystal Clarity, 1946.

REFERENCES

[illegible] "The case for multi-channel learning". In [illegible] (ed.) [illegible] Learning: [illegible]. Washington D.C.: [illegible], 199[illegible].

[illegible] National Strategies of e-Learning, Paris: IIEP, 2002.

Blanchard, Ken and Others, Whale Done, London: Nicholas Brealey, 2002.

Bloom, Benjamin, Taxonomy of Educational Objectives: The Classification of Educational Goals, Handbook II: Affective Domain, New York: David McKay, 1956.

Chopra, D., Ageless Body, Timeless Mind, London: Rider, 1993.

Lal, Santosh K., The Educational System of [illegible], New Delhi: [illegible], 198[illegible].

Dyer, W.W., Your Erroneous Zones, New York: Harper Collins, 1995. Gardner, Howard, Frames of Mind: The Theory of Multiple Intelligences, London: [illegible], 1993.

Gibran, K., The Prophet, New Delhi: UBSPD, 1997.

Goleman, D., Emotional Intelligence, London: Bantam, 1995.

[illegible]

[illegible] New York: [illegible], 197[illegible].

[illegible] New Delhi: Macmillan, 1998.

[illegible] California [illegible], 199[illegible].

[illegible] New Delhi: [illegible].

Mukhopadhyay, M. and [illegible], [illegible] Analysis as [illegible] Teacher Classroom Behaviour [illegible] 1982 [illegible].

[illegible]

[illegible] Multi-channel Learning Systems [illegible] 2001.

[illegible]

[illegible]

[illegible]

[illegible]